STEEPLE · BOOKS

This series offers the concerned reader basic guidelines and *practical* applications of religion for today's world. Although decidedly Christian in focus and emphasis, the series embraces all denominations and modes of Bible-based belief relevant to our lives today. All volumes in the Steeple series are originals, freshly written to provide a fresh perspective on current—and yet timeless—human dilemmas. This is a series for our times. Among the books:

How to Read the Bible
James Fischer

How to Live Your Faith
L. Perry Wilbur

A Spiritual Handbook for Women
Dandi Daley Knorr

Temptation: How Christians Can Deal with It
Frances Carroll

*With God on Your Side: A Guide to Finding
Self-Worth Through Total Faith*
Doug Manning

*A Daily Key for Today's Christians:
365 Key Texts of the New Testament*
William E. Bowles

*Walking in the Garden:
Inner Peace from the Flowers of God*
Paula Connor

How to Bring Up Children in the Catholic Faith
Carol and David Powell

*Sex in the Bible: An Introduction to
What the Scriptures Teach Us About Sexuality*
Michael R. Cosby

*How to Talk with God Every Day of the Year:
A Book of Devotions for Twelve Positive Months*
Frances Hunter

*God's Conditions for Prosperity:
How to Earn the Rewards of Christian Living*
Charles Hunter

*Pilgrimages: A Guide to the Holy Places
of Europe for Today's Traveler*
Paul Lambourne Higgins

*Journey into the Light: Lessons of Pain and Joy
to Renew Your Energy and Strengthen Your Faith*
Dorris Blough Murdock

Prentice-Hall International, Inc., *London*
Prentice-Hall of Australia Pty. Limited, *Sydney*
Prentice-Hall Canada Inc., *Toronto*
Prentice-Hall of India Private Limited, *New Delhi*
Prentice-Hall of Japan, Inc., *Tokyo*
Prentice-Hall of Southeast Asia Pte. Ltd., *Singapore*
Whitehall Books Limited, *Wellington, New Zealand*
Editora Prentice-Hall do Brasil Ltda., *Rio de Janeiro*

Stuart Litvak and Nora Burba

IN THE WORLD BUT NOT OF IT

A Guide to More Spirituality in Your Life

A SPECTRUM BOOK

Prentice-Hall, Inc., Englewood Cliffs, New Jersey 07632

Library of Congress Cataloging in Publication Data

Litvak, Stuart.
    In the world but not of it.

    (Steeple books)
    "A Spectrum Book."
    Bibliography: p.
    Includes index.
    1. Spirituality.   I. Burba, Nora.   II. Title.
III. Series.
BV4501.2.L57 1984   248.4   84-11656
ISBN 0-13-454000-X
ISBN 0-13-453994-X (pbk.)

For Jane, Bill, and Christy Manley

A SPECTRUM BOOK

10   9   8   7   6   5   4   3   2   1

Printed in the United States of America

ISBN 0-13-454000-X

ISBN 0-13-453994-X {PBK.}

Cover design by Hal Siegel

This book is available at a special discount when ordered in
bulk quantities. Contact Prentice-Hall, Inc., General
Publishing Division, Special Sales, Englewood Cliffs, N.J. 07632.

contents

chapter one
the spiritual self
1

chapter two
who comes first?
9

chapter three
is it worth dying for?
15

chapter four
at whose expense?
26

chapter five
good humor
33

chapter six
spirituality in action
43

chapter seven
world as illusion
53

chapter eight
brotherhood/sisterhood
63

chapter nine
words and practice
72

chapter ten
to be human again
79

chapter eleven
creative consciousness
86

chapter twelve
service
95

chapter thirteen
consciousness evolving
99

further reading
117

index
120

preface

One couple faithfully attends Bible study in their small town each Wednesday evening. A recently divorced man joins a counseling group to help him sort out his feelings. A business major in a large university regularly signs up for philosophy and humanities classes. These people have one thing in common—in their own way, they are searching for meaning. Whether they know it or not, they are involved in a spiritual quest.

In an important book, *The Unconscious God,* psychiatrist Viktor Frankl surmises that "man's search for meaning" is the highest and most unique quality of being a human. He conceives religion, as he describes it, in "the widest possible sense," as the human need to find an answer to the ultimate question: "What is the meaning of life?" By viewing religion within this broad perspective, Frankl notes that this brings religion into all areas of everyday life and human activity.

Hence, religion as conceived by Frankl is not simply a creed that one is expected to believe in, or a denomination, church, or synagogue. Religion, in this broader meaning of spirituality, is not simply attending services regularly and adhering to one's set of preferred beliefs. True spirituality does not operate in a vacuum. It is engaging in real life. When operative, it is capable of altering your behavior, attitudes, perceptions, and values.

In this age of economic difficulties, political unrest, environmental destruction, pollution, traffic, overcrowding, stress, drug abuse, war, and the threat of nuclear devastation, the effort to lead a spiritually oriented life is seen as more essential than ever. Reading the Bible or listening to a sermon can be useful to some extent, but history has proven that these alone are not sufficient, that these approaches to the alteration of human nature do not penetrate deeply enough. Psychological research has shown that for human behavior to change, what is required (in addition to information) is insight, experience, and personal effort.

Our prime motive in writing this book is to assist you in the endeavor—to suggest and provoke—of bridging the gap between religious theory and spiritual reality. And, we hope that it will be something you can apply to your everyday circumstances, to your relationships, to your work, and to your family life.

May your quest be successful.

Many thanks to Wayne Senzee for his editorial assistance, and to Jane Manley for typing the manuscript and procuring the copyright permissions. We are grateful to our editor, Mary Kennan, who, as always, has been a great source of encouragement and support. Her assistant, Stephanie Kiriakopoulos, has been very helpful, as has our production editor, Eric Newman. Not least, LaJeane Shearer was most generous in providing us with helpful research materials.

We also wish to thank the authors, publishers, and authors' representatives listed below for permission to use the following selections:

Excerpt from *Earthwalk* by Philip Slater. Copyright © 1974 by Philip Slater. Reprinted by permission of Doubleday & Company, Inc.

The quotation on page 33 is from Woody Allen, *Getting Even*. Copyright © 1978 by Woody Allen. It is reprinted by permission of Random House, Inc., and Woody Allen.

Excerpt from "Automated Lives" by Ellen J. Langer, *Psychology Today*, April 1982. Reprinted from *Psychology Today* magazine, copyright © 1982 (APA).

Excerpt from "Ethics without the sermon" by Laura L. Nash, *Harvard Business Review*, November–December 1981. Reprinted by permission of the *Harvard Business Review*. Copyright © 1981 by the President and Fellows of Harvard College; all rights reserved.

Excerpt from *Simulations of God* by John Lilly, New York, Bantam, 1975. Copyright © 1956, 1958, 1960, 1961, 1969, 1975 by John Lilly, M.D. All rights reserved.

Excerpt reprinted from *Tales of the Hasidim: Later Masters* by Martin Buber. Copyright © 1948 by Schocken Books Inc.

Excerpt reprinted from *Ten Rungs: Hasidic Sayings,* collected and edited by Martin Buber. Copyright 1947 by Schocken Books Inc. Copyright © 1975 renewed by Schocken Books Inc.

chapter one

the spiritual self

*The true harvest of my daily life is somewhat as intangible and as
indescribable as the tints of morning and evening. It is a little
star-dust caught, a segment of the rainbow which I have clutched.*

—HENRY DAVID THOREAU

The word *spiritual* is rarely heard in the vernacular these
days. We used to hear it, ten or fifteen years ago, as in "Oh
wow, he's real spiritual, man," referring to the rich college
drop-out who blew his trust fund traveling to India learning
the latest mantras. Currently, it is a label many of us nerv-
ously avoid because it seems to have connotations of (1)
calling up vaporous visits from long-deceased ancestors, (2)
Born-Again babblings, or (3) social intercourse with small
green men from outer space.

But spirituality is a quality that all of us share—to be
fully human is to be spiritual. And in these fast-paced decades, it is an asset that we should understand and expand
upon.

In our modern western society, the idea of spirituality
has become fairly secularized, associated in many people's
minds with public and highly visible "good deeds." We see
the extremes of this in politics and "civic pride." We should

1

learn, however, to distinguish between real charity or self-lessness and that form of it that is mere self-aggrandizement, be it ever so cultivated. The following story makes the distinction clear.

The uppercrust of a certain town sponsored an annual program and banquet called the "Citizen of the Year" award. It was a custom of the fete for the mayor and council members of a neighboring city to each make an informal visit to this town sometime during the year to observe the achievements of the several hopefuls for the prestigious honor. They later submitted to their counterparts the name of the winner.

One former recipient of this prize was a woman who happened to be very highly placed in the social register and who tirelessly gave of her time and energy to each and every charity and community-improvement project—in short, a veritable city saint dynamo. Her picture appeared regularly in the society pages of the local newspaper.

Ironically, but not really so improbably, this woman's husband was a notorious town drunkard. One might think that such a man would be a fatal societal blight on the reputation of his wifely paragon. He was, in fact, the reverse. Almost everyone considered her a martyr for keeping him and suffering with him—much like taking in and enduring a devilish orphan. The contrast made her even brighter.

The preparations for this year's ceremony went, as usual, very much according to plan, and the aforementioned municipal matron was once again the heavy favorite to waltz off with the emblazoned plaque.

It so happened, however, that this time the newly elected mayor who headed the observation team was a wise man, and his council members were sincere seekers of truth.

The long-awaited evening arrived, and the local mayor

introduced the guest officials with more than a little eloquence and pomp. At last his mayoral counterpart stood up.

"Honorable mayor, distinguished citizens of this fair town. After due observation and assessment of the public works and personal merits of the various candidates for this award, we elect, to a man, the only possible recipient of it." One hundred heads turned toward the expected shoo-in.

"Understandably, however, he has not graced us with his presence tonight . . ." The same number of jaws fell open. ". . . Mr. Henry Smith, a most notable and worthy resident of your community and husband, I believe, of last year's winner and some years before that . . ."

Most of the audience thought, of course, that this mayor could himself win a prize for bad taste and humor. But the speaker continued.

"Most of you think I am making a poor joke. On the contrary. For overwhelming reasons, Mr. Smith is indeed our choice for this honor."

The host mayor sprang to his feet. "Sir, this is an outrage! We of this community take this program very seriously! You had better have a good explanation for this insult!"

"Indeed I have," answered the speaker, "although it is not presented as an insult. We, your civic neighbors, take this competition as seriously as do you. For covetousness and vanity are contagious and might infect our town as deeply as it has yours. It has been truly said that 'greed for higher things is still greed.' So it is for all the eager seekers of such trophies everywhere. Such greed is no less contagious when it is communalized in the form of preening for recognition of 'good works' . . .

"Mr. Smith was chosen because he is in fact a good man who demonstrates a complete lack of the trait that is so prevalent among you—an addiction to applause. His virtue

3

of true generosity, charity, kindliness, and humility are known only to the unfortunate of this town, whom he continually and anonymously gave of himself. Therefore, he is an impeccable standard for everyone here in the aspect of community improvement."

And that is the essence of spirituality. This also defines what spirituality is *not*—religiosity or outward piety. So, if you were expecting mantras or some mild Bible thumping, put this book back on the shelf and go on to another tome. In this book, we make a rather significant distinction between spirituality and religion. Spirituality refers to the spirit or soul—to the higher consciousness within all of us. It is, as Mr. Webster defines it, our "animating vapor." Religion, on the other hand, is defined by Webster as the "belief in a divine or superhuman power to be obeyed and worshipped as the creator(s) and ruler(s) of the universe . . . expression of this belief in conduct and ritual . . . any specific system of belief, worship, conduct, etc., often involving a code of ethics and philosophy: as, the Christian *religion,* the Buddhist *religion,* etc. . . . any object of conscientious regard and pursuit: as, cleanliness was a religion to him."

We don't mean to devalue religion. It has some very important functions in all cultures. But we want to get beyond the ritualistic, compulsive, culturally ingrained aspects of religion and delve into the higher sense of spirituality—our natural inheritance that links us across cultures and across time. Interestingly, religion is something that is drilled into our heads by our culture, and spirituality is subtly whisked out like an unwanted encyclopedia salesman or some vaporous and unneeded guest. In order to make it difficult for spirituality to thrive in our modern western culture, we are rewarded for our nonspiritual practices, such as greedily competing with our fellow man for social stature and material goods. These base mate-

4

rial values then spawn more antispiritual tendencies such as jealousy, selfishness, and envy.

In his book, *Simulations of God,* Dr. John Lilly clearly illustrates how our spiritual orientation towards God can become displaced into a religious obsession with idols. Our idols can include such things as preoccupation with food, having sex, getting high frequently, war, Warren Beatty, and video games. In this view, even atheism (the belief in no God) and agnosticism (the belief that one doesn't know if there is a God or not) can be forms of religion—that is, a belief or set of beliefs that one "religiously" or obsessively adheres to. Hence, Madelyn Murray O'Hare, the head of the atheism movement in the United States, may, in this light, be seen as a "religious" leader.

Along these same lines, someone who calls himself a Christian yet does not obey Christianity's tenets cannot be regarded as a Christian. On the other hand, someone who doesn't believe he or she has a religion yet relies on astrology or numerology can be considered of that "religion." Basically, religion pertains to the beliefs by which one lives: one's religion can (unknowingly) be one's corporation, one's life-consuming hobby (such as stamp collecting), or one's nation and its Constitution, and can also be the commonly known philosophies such as hedonism or stoicism as well as the psychological schools of thought such as behaviorism, psychoanalysis, and existentialism. Even lifelong pessimism or optimism can contain religious overtones.

Spirituality does *not* involve obsession, beliefs, or compulsion. It is considered a mode, essence, or experience that resides deep in the human mind, waiting to be activated. A spiritual action, therefore, is seen as one that spontaneously arises as the result of a natural humanizing impulse. It is saying "I love you" to someone and really meaning it, as opposed to saying that phrase daily to your spouse at precisely 8:15 a.m. as you stride through the door on your way out. That's about as spiritual (and loving) as brushing your teeth twice a day.

The good news is that spirituality is something that can be cultivated—but not indoctrinated—like a flower that blooms as the result of the right amounts of sunshine, pruning, fertilizer, and water. Spirituality is something that can unfold or grow; it is related to higher development.

It follows from all this that whereas a spiritual or developed person may also be religious (he or she may attend church and celebrate certain religious holidays), it does not necessarily follow that a religious person is spiritual. Religion, then, can be quite insular. A religious person may attend church or synagogue regularly, may read or memorize the Bible, may obey religious rituals and holidays, and may wear special jewelry or garments. That person will also normally subscribe to a special set of beliefs or practices that are sometimes at odds with other religions or beliefs. This is why there are religious wars.

Spirituality, however, runs deeper. Truly spiritual people are rarely at odds because they share the same innate human capacities and fulfillments. Spiritual people are essentially transformed. Their lower or animal tendencies have been tamed or harnessed, not bullwhipped, into useful productivity. Many religious people are essentially untransformed. Their lower or animal selves have merely been temporarily suppressed by a set of ritualistic beliefs and practices.

Two recent studies, one psychological and one sociological, make these matters quite clear. Citing his study of a large group of churchgoers, the psychologist William Eckhards concluded, "Compassion was not consistent with conventional religiosity . . . [as] conceived and practiced in our culture today" and "compassionate theists are in the minority . . . in the Western world today."[1] There was no correlation in this study between religion and compassion (a spiritual impulse). In another study, sociologist James A. Christenson found that "people who regularly attend church exhibit no greater social compassion than those who do not attend."[2]

Being religious is something that only seems to crop up at certain prescribed moments of life, such as when you're at your local Bible study meeting or contemplating God in the Temple. Spirituality, however, can manifest itself in the smallest of ways, in the oddest moments. A young boy lovingly petting his dog is being "spiritual"; a man stopping to help someone on the highway is spiritual; holding the elevator door for someone is, in some sense, being spiritual.

Spirituality requires no chanting, no elaborate buildings designed by famous architects, and no removal of self from daily activities. If you're spiritual, you can still use public restrooms. It does not mean mouthing pieties or attempting conversions. It is recognizing and coming to terms with our own base self, our greed, vanity, arrogance, selfishness, temper, jealousy, envy, hatred, prejudice, hypocrisy, deceit, animosities, and hostilities. Spirituality is the total of the efforts made in this direction and the development and manifestations of our higher self—the ability to love, sympathize, show compassion, and care for others, our honesty and sincerity, our sense of justice, and our desire to serve. Spiritually oriented people *are*. They manifest *being*. Their spirituality is within. It is an inner attainment. However it often manifests overtly in the form of good deeds. These deeds are not just done for social approval or to escape punishment. They are accomplished simply by the operation of insight and understanding on the part of the person involved. Many spiritual good deeds are done anonymously.

Spiritual impulses and deeds happen all the time, usually without much thinking. But we need to concentrate, to reflect, and to make these deeds and impulses a more frequent aspect of our lives. We must understand spirituality as a life-sustaining and life-elevating process. Maybe the world won't turn into the last reel of a Shirley Temple film, but we all may become a bit more compassionate and human. This book is designed to inform and assist you in all these objectives.

NOTES

1   Eckhardt, William. *Compassion: Toward a Science of Value.* Toronto: CPRI Press, 1973, pp. 265, 262.
2   Christenson, James A. "Religious Involvement, Values and Social Compassion," *Sociological Analysis,* 1976, 37, p. 218.

chapter two

who comes first?

*It's not love we should have painted as
blind, but self-love.*
—VOLTAIRE

We work out on Nautilus equipment and regularly attend
our exercise classes. We buy ourselves Rolex watches as
rewards and treat ourselves to double scoops of Häagen-
Dazs ice cream when we have a bad day. We are rubbed,
scrubbed, and indulged. Nowadays, our slogan seems to be:
"If *I* don't pamper myself, *nobody* will."

Naturally, we are conscientious, aware, and sensitive
types; we do suffer a bit of spiritual guilt over our narcissistic ways. Judith Viorst, in her book *Love and Guilt and the
Meaning of Life,* sums it up wittily when she defines this
spiritual angst as "Praying, instead of for peace on earth,
that your hair will look terrific tomorrow morning."

We have passed from the age of the rugged individual
and of the Protestant work ethic into the era of mass narcissism. The concept of loving thy neighbor has shrunk into
loving thyself most. Naturally, we rationalize it by noting
that we can't love anyone else until we learn to love our own
selves. True—but only to a point.

Narcissism, which was described as early as 1898 as

auto-eroticism by psychologist Havelock Ellis, is commonly thought of as a personality disorder in psychiatric circles. It's characterized by self-absorption or an obsession with one's self. But, then, almost everyone's like that these days. Does that mean that our entire "Me Generation" has one mass personality disorder? Maybe so. It does seem to be the norm. In his perceptive book, *Earthwalk,* author Philip Slater draws an analogy between our society's narcissism and cancer. He uses the term *social metastasis* to refer to the unbridled growth and spread of highly individualistic "cancer" cells. "Studies of cancer cells seem to suggest that some kind of mutually limiting communication present between normal cells is weak or absent between cancer cells. It is as if cancer cells had been heavily indoctrinated with the ideology of overindividualism and personal achievement."[1]

In today's popular culture, our tendency to arrogantly *metastasize* is constantly reinforced. Why is it wrong, when practically everything we read and see tells us it's okay? Flip through popular magazines at the checkout counter and you will find articles such as "Character Push-ups: How To Build The Four Personality Skills That Get You To The Top," "18 Exercises to Speed Up Body Sleekness," and "Clothes Confidence: How To Find the Hidden Promise in Your Looks." Self-help books such as *Getting Even, Self Creation,* and *How to Win Friends and Influence People* sell like cold Perrier in the middle of the Sahara. Advertisers coax us into losing weight, gaining fresh-breath confidence, fighting underarm wetness, and surrendering to the lure of mink. Is it any wonder we spend more time preening before a mirror than we do contemplating hunger and impoverishment in the world?

In a 1979 survey on the subject of friendship, *Psychology Today* asked their readers "Who are our friends—and what do we expect of them?" Over 40,000 readers sent in replies to 64 questions, with a key question being "How important to you is each of these qualities in a friend?" The highest percentage listed "keeps confidences" (89%), "loyalty" (88%), "warmth, affection" (81%), "supportiveness" (76%), "frankness" (75%), "sense of humor" (75%), and "willingness to make time for me," (62%). Interestingly, none of the questions asked of the readers inquired as to what sort of qualities *they* had to offer their friends.

The extent to which self-aggrandizement has infiltrated our society is best revealed in Christopher Lasch's *The Culture of Narcissism.* Lasch notes that not only is narcissism prominent in awareness movements and cults, "but is also present in business corporations, political organizations, and government bureaucracies. For all his inner suffering, the narcissist has many traits that make for success in bureaucratic institutions, which put a premium on the manipulation of interpersonal relations, discourage the formation of deep personal attachment, and at the same time provide the narcissist with the approval he needs in order to validate his self-esteem."[2] Lasch also reveals the presence of self-absorption in such "institutions" as sports (win at all cost), education (as "commodity" instead of process), and the family (overindulgence of the child by narcissistic parents).

Lasch (as well as other scholars and writers) sees this new narcissism as a form of overcompensation. According to this particular theory, it's a way for people to deal with the pathology of the times. This pathology is characterized by a sense of inner emptiness resulting from fragmentation— the loss of connectiveness or emotional commitment to the community. Narcissism supposedly functions to fill the vacuum.

Other popular writers, such as Tom Wolfe, Marilyn Ferguson, and Alvin Toffler, tend to take a different, positive view of our current tendency toward self-absorption. They seem to feel that this narcissism movement is merely an "evolutionary" stage toward what Toffler describes as the "Third Wave" and what Wolfe describes as the "Third Great Awakening." They believe that this trend will lead to personal and social maturity, growth and transformation.

11

In other words, our society is not heading toward individualistic ruin and disaster; rather, we will come full circle once we get to know ourselves.

Theodore Roszak also sees this awareness movement in a positive light. In his talk to the World Symposium on Humanity in 1977, Roszak spoke confidently of the Manifesto of the Person—"the declaration of our sovereign right of self-discovery." He further adds, "We may come to see that tribe, nation, class, that social movement, historical necessity, have all, like shadows that eclipse the sun, gained their existence at the expense of something far brighter and more beautiful—our essential and still unexplored self." Roszak is not so naive as to not realize the narcissistic elements in the Manifesto. He is aware that self-preoccupation may accompany the movement, so he makes a clear distinction between the *individual* and the *person:* ". . . it is the individual who has, in our society, distorted our conception of the self. So to be concerned with one's self has come to mean vanity, deceit, selfishness . . . It has meant proving one's qualities at the expense of others; playing the game to win." But this, according to Roszak, is the result, not of the spiritual search for self-discovery, but of "competitive middle-class demands of social morality . . . It is therefore as much anti-personal as it is anti-social." On the other hand, he views the search for the person as "quiet exploration, undertaken in candor and curiosity; its aim is neither success nor celebrity, but self-knowledge . . . the joy of the quest does not lie in working up those competitive energies that allow us to triumph over others. The search is for those qualities we share with others, and for the uniqueness, which raises us above all competition."[3]

So this *Me Generation* can be seen from several angles. It all seems to hinge on motives. If you are involved in the movement—in learning about yourself—merely for selfish purposes (such as getting ahead at the expense of others or to make yourself look chic and aware in the eyes of your peers), your motive could easily be labeled as anti-social or anti-spiritual. If your honest motive is self-discovery or self-understanding, and by doing so you become an asset to others, then your involvement is healthy, even spiritual. The distinction is as subtle as a wink at an auction—but just as essential and important.

Encouragingly, we *are* seeing the faint glimmers of the *We* or *Us* Decade. We are starting to learn that people who are too wound up in themselves usually wind up with the television screen as their only companion. Tolerance and tact, once banished to the "cop-out" closet are creeping back into use. Brutal honesty and self-righteousness ("Your breath would kill a toad at two miles, and I'm going to tell you about it because otherwise I would be a bad and deceptive person . . .") have been found to sever more relationships than start them (who wants to listen to that kind of abuse anyway?). Marriage, families, parents, babies, best friends, and volunteer work are suddenly okay again. Open marriage seems to work well only for divorce lawyers.

On the other hand, this *usness* shouldn't be carried out to the nth degree either—a balance is necessary. To much *usness* can produce a society of lemmings—cultists and conformists—who trundle over cliffs just because someone says so. We could go to the extremes of Jim Jones and his brainwashed band of Kool-Aid quaffers, or the very scary Reverend Moon, who set up and married several thousand of his glassy-eyed followers (the brides were resplendent in their identical Simplicity pattern gowns).

Thus, the me/us line is svelte indeed. We do have a sovereign right to self-discovery, and we do have an obligation to others on our same patch of land. But we must see both sides of this awareness for all of us to move forward in the direction of higher spirituality.

NOTES

1   Slater, Philip, *Earthwalk*. New York: Bantam, 1974, p. 44.
2   Lasch, Christopher, *The Culture of Narcissism*. New York: W. W. Norton & Company, Inc., New York, N.Y., 1979.
3   Roszak, Theodore, *Person/Planet*. Doubleday & Co., 1978.

chapter three

is it worth dying for?

What does it profit a man
if he gains the whole world
but loses his own soul?
—JESUS

He is the ideal American male—successful, handsome, prosperous. His 22-year marriage to his high-school sweetheart has produced two outstanding daughters, both honor students in their high school. They live in a high-income neighborhood, drive expensive cars, and can afford life's other pleasures. He and his wife are health and exercise conscious. He is a cardiologist—highly respected in his field—and has written many articles and a book on heart disease. He is frequently on the road, addressing groups on this subject.

In January 1972, while lecturing to the American Academy of Family Physicians on how to prevent heart attacks, he—Dr. Robert S. Eliot—felt a tightening of the chest. He had a heart attack. He was 44.

Eliot, now fully recovered and practicing in Phoenix, Arizona, was not your typical heart attack candidate. Prior to his coronary, he really believed that he was immune to heart disease. He didn't smoke, he wasn't overweight. He didn't have high cholesterol or diabetes, and there was no history of heart disease in his family. All of the physiological traits were good.

But Eliot did exhibit one fatal trait, a trait that now is being considered as a major risk factor in heart disease: his self-destructive personality and lifestyle. Today, more and more heart disease is being found in younger (thirties and forties), "strappingly healthy" Americans.

Looking back, Eliot sheds some light on his past behavior patterns. "My life had been a blur of overachievement to gain recognition," he remembers. When some of his high aspirations seemed to be a bit out of reach, he says he "picked up the pace, I tried to force things through, I had no time for friends and family, relaxation, and diversion. . . . I had become locked in a joyless struggle. I was being softened for the blow."

Eliot was lucky enough to have lived and benefitted from the terrifying experience of the heart attack. ". . . the last eight years have been the best of my life. The insights I gained while staring into the abyss of death have helped me to face up to stress and make it a friend, not foe."[1]

As we mentioned, Dr. Eliot was not alone as one of those "strappingly healthy" Americans who suddenly keel over with a heart attack. In fact, researchers are discovering that in more than half of all new cases of heart disease, none of the usual risk factors (smoking, lack of exercise, history of heart disease, etc.) is present.[2] So there is that growing consensus among investigators that our weird behavior patterns are jamming our electrical systems.

Right about now, you may be wondering why we're focusing upon heart disease. This is supposed to be a book about spirituality, right? Exactly. If more people were spiritually inclined, perhaps there would be fewer people keeling over dead from behavior-induced coronaries. However, welcome to the *Age of Angina*. Our modern, fast-paced society is rampantly breeding more and more coronary cases.

But let's bring this disease back down to the individual level. (We'll tackle the social/cultural factors in a bit.) The best-known research to reveal the link between psychological/behavioral factors and heart disease was done by Drs. Meyer Friedman and Ray Rosenman and was summarized in their best-selling book, *Type A Behavior and Your Heart.* Their research has led them to conclude that,

> *In the absence of Type A Behavior Pattern, coronary heart disease never occurs before seventy years of age, regardless of the fatty foods eaten, the cigarettes smoked, or the lack of exercise. But when this behavior pattern is present, coronary heart disease can easily erupt in one's thirties and forties.*[3]

What is this Type A behavior? Many of you have probably heard of it by now. Essentially, the doctors have isolated two general behavior patterns: Type A and Type B. And it's the A's who are getting most of the press. People who have Type A behavior generally exhibit ". . . excessive competitive drive, aggressiveness, impatience, and a harrying sense of time urgency. Individuals displaying this pattern seem to be engaged in a chronic, ceaseless, and often fruitless struggle—with themselves, with others, with circumstances, with time, sometimes with life itself. They also frequently exhibit a free-floating but well-rationalized form of hostility, and almost always a deep-seated insecurity."[4] We all know somebody like that (perhaps ourselves), who, for example, pushes through college, lands a great job, pushes for promotions, moves around to further career goals, joins a trillion organizations to make the "right" contacts, and is always in a hurry. It's rare that they take a two-hour lunch unless it's with an important client.

The researchers have found that Type A behavior exists in different degrees in different individuals, but is especially common among urban Americans. In one major study of 2500 Federal employees in the San Francisco area, 50 to 60 percent were found to be authentic Type A's, and about 10 percent were extreme cases (and you thought that government bureaucrats were dour, grayfaced, and worked at a snail's pace!). In their investigation, the researchers also uncovered a behavior pattern quite the opposite of Type A that they dubbed Type B. Type B's are people "who felt no sense of time urgency, exhibited no excessive competitive drive or free-floating hostility."

Friedman and Rosenman then address themselves to the key question: Why are Type A (and Type B) people the way they are and why do they behave the way they do? The researchers cite several reasons, all that seem to suggest that Type A people (as opposed to Type B people) are, above all, extremely greedy. They are greedy for possessions, money, power, status, and achievement. As part of this pattern they tend to live in the fast lane, they are usually in a hurry (Friedman and Rosenman refer to this as "hurry sickness," or a "habitual sense of time urgency"), and they tend to be workaholics.

Type A's are usually highly competitive, even when they needn't be. For example, our typical Type A will decide to take up the recreational sport of waterskiing. Rather than just learning it and enjoying the activity for what it's worth, Type A will push him or herself to master the sport almost to the point of professionalism. Then all he or she needs to do is move to Florida, wear tutus and ski for the tourists. Type A's also tend to overreact. Dr. Eliot refers to these heart-attack-prone people as "hot reactors" who are distinguished by a triad of "hostility, impatience and competitiveness." A Type A, then, will brood, scream, mope and gripe if he or she is overlooked for a promotion. They don't tend to shrug things off easily. But as a way to combat this triad of self-destructiveness, Eliot always reminds his heart patients of the risks: "Is it worth dying for?" Eliot, as well as Friedman and Rosenman, utilizes a series of lifestyle management strategies as a means of helping his patients change their ways. While these strategies (such as slowing down, learning how to relax, rechanneling hostilities, etc.) are useful, they are only partially helpful. While Friedman and Rosenman recognize (and discuss in two pages) the Type A's "fascination with the quantitative accumulation of material objects," the key problem of greed needs to be better understood and dealt with.

Greed. It's not only the greed for money or material goods that we are discussing as the root of Type A behavior, but a greed for time, for achievement, for recognition—for power. And this greed stunts our spiritual growth. On the larger scale, it is the cause of many national and global problems such as economic, political and social crises. Greed is unquestionably the mental malignancy of our time. How could it be otherwise when we have a culture that worships wealth, power, and achievement?

Not only does this impulse or motive underlie many of our individual actions, but it also affects virtually every one of our national institutions. Greed and power permeate such institutions as science, education, the media, political parties, government, business, labor, and even religion. In the area of religion, people are constantly trying to convince themselves and others that *their* religion is best, that *their* scriptures are correct, that *their* church is the better one to attend, that *they* must spread the word. Whereas *missions* may at one time (long ago) have been spiritually and purely motivated, the hidden greed, power, and self-righteousness in many missionaries is apparent. Such missions (including door-to-door proselytizing) often take on an obsessive/compulsive quality that is typically a sign of power seeking or even pathology.

Writer Philip Slater has a special gift for insight into the workings of greed in society as a whole, which is best reflected in his book *Earthwalk* and a superb article entitled "Wealth Addiction" (*Quest,* November/December, 1977). What Slater has noticed is that wealth addiction is not only

19

destructive (ultimately to all of us) and tantamount to mental illness, but that it is *culturally sanctioned*. While both idealists and conservatives might, if questioned, wish to deny it, wealth addiction is wholly encouraged throughout most of the Western world, especially in the U.S. The accumulation of wealth and abundant material possessions are proof of success in the Great American Dream. Our heroes are almost invariably the wealthy—movie stars, sports greats, political figures, business leaders. We eagerly read and hear about singer Kenny Rogers' wife, who *simply* could not find a decent house with a pool and tennis court with the million or so dollar budget Kenny had given her (imagine that!). Or there's Malcolm Forbes, who collects jeweled eggs like most people collect mosquito bites in a swamp and who entertains famous celebrities aboard his little ol' million-dollar yacht. We're fascinated with wealth and the wealthy, and everywhere we turn, the signals for us to pursue our own means to wealth are there.

Slater notes, however, that most often, the wealthy are rarely satisfied—they always want more. Slater refers to wealth and power addicts as *plutomaniacs,* which he defines as those with a "morbid craving for wealth." He also goes on to point out that such addicts (and, admittedly, there's some of this addiction in everyone) are almost never fulfilled. Most of all, Slater reasons, plutomaniacs are a menace to practically everyone else, since the overaccumulation of wealth by one person deprives (and causes pain to) many other persons.

On the larger, global scale, greed has developed into all sorts of "cancerous" forms, and, recalling Slater's idea of *social metastasis,* it is clearly and largely (but unknowingly to most) entangled in and responsible for, the modern, pathological obsession and trend towards "growth": "The kind of growth Western culture has experienced over the past 300 years would be considered a sign of gross malfunction in any other context. Healthy growth is paced differently—it does not absorb or destroy everything living around it. It is cancerous cells that grow and reproduce rapidly in total disregard of their connection with surrounding cells . . . our task here is to understand the origin of the growth delusion, how it took hold of us so violently, how it ramifies through our thought processes, and how to eradicate it."[5] By growth, Slater is referring to overpopulation, the obsession with technology in lieu of human concerns, economic growth (causing runaway inflation, recessions, and ecological disregard), and the information explosion (with the subsequent lack of *understanding* this information).

Slater's position is well reflected elsewhere, in such fine books as *The End of Affluence* (Paul Ehrlich), *The Coming Dark Age* (Roberto Vacca), and *Human Scale* (Kirkpatrick Sale). In these and several other books, the authors attempt, at times, to provide solutions, however most of these solutions do not take the *Human*—or more specifically human psychology—into sufficient consideration. Solutions tend to be economic, political, ecological, technological, strategic, etc. Few of these writers acknowledge the core of the problem(s): human nature, and more specifically, greed.

So what can we do about greed, that evil that lurks within us? First of all, we must better understand the nature and manifestations of greed, and, secondly, we must stare at ourselves in the mirror without posing and acknowledging the dollar signs dancing around in our eyes. In varying degrees and in varying situations, we are all greedy. We may not always be conscious of it, but it may motivate us in our daily actions. (Have you ever been slow to pick up a lunch tab but quick to be in line when a department store is handing out free samples of something?) Greed may motivate us in our major life decisions such as marriage. Why do people get married? Sure, love is the conscious and correct answer, but deep down, aren't there factors such as greediness for security, your mate's possessions or position, approval from peers, attention, reputation, or money? Are we greedy to have babies? If we would question our motives a bit more, perhaps fewer marriages would fail.

This reflection, this same sort of questioning should take place in our lives on a daily basis. Perhaps then we'll learn to deal with our greed. Why do you work where you work? That's an important question. Why do we spend hours charting, plotting, and analyzing sex, but so little time actually making love? Why do we spend hundreds of dollars on cookbooks and gourmet cooking classes, only to whip through dinner in 45 minutes because of an important evening meeting? Why do we spend hours shopping for exciting new ensembles, when in reality, there are only so many clothes that are necessary to make it through an average week?

Coming full circle, if you're a medical doctor, or more specifically, a cardiologist, why do you want to publish 200 journal articles, travel 100 days a year all over the country to give lectures, and then get upset when your name isn't mentioned in the latest issue of *Time* magazine that is featuring an article on heart disease?

Is it worth dying for?

Greed seems to be one of the leading causes of death, personal and social destruction, and pain. However, greed can be understood better and either controlled, or (better) transformed. Control is sometimes useful, but basically this is often only mere suppression and either causes stress or sublimation (manifested in "approved" activities that only *seem* not to be fueled by greed). And very often the controls weaken, the stored greed gushing out in the form of binges or inappropriate or blatantly unbecoming behavior (picture a dieter set loose in an ice cream warehouse). In an effort to transform greed into a positive force or to neutralize it, one needs to gain greater self- and other-insight and needs to become more generally aware or conscious. This is part of the spiritual or developmental quest. To begin, you might wish to better understand the distinction between *being* and *having*. You might wish to contemplate—not merely read or even memorize—the following:

> *For whosoever will save his life shall lose it; but whosoever will lose his life for my sake, the same shall save it. For what is a man advantaged, if he gain the whole world and lose himself, or be cast away?*

—LUKE 9:24-25

This is what Jesus, as well as other great spiritual leaders, taught, and it reflects on the dual meaning of the notion *to have. To have,* as the opposite of *to be,* means to hold or possess things: material objects, power, your body, people, etc. *To be* means freedom from want, implying the positive inner state of *being* which means you *have* in the sense that you *have* everything (wholeness) without *having* (accumulating) anything. Erich Fromm, in his book *To Have Or To Be?* boldly states that, ". . . empirical anthropological and psychoanalytic data tend to demonstrate that *having and being are true fundamental modes of experience, the respective strengths of which determine the differences between the characters and various types of social character.*"[6] He strongly holds that this distinction between having and being (together with the distinction between love of life and love of the dead) "represents the most crucial problem of existence." By *love of life,* Fromm means that those who *are* and who can *be,* are not afraid of dying. To be afraid to die, in his view, is connected with the *having* mode. Because when you die, you think you will lose all that you have. Those not in the *being* mode but more in the *having* mode are actually in *love of the dead* in the sense that they are preoccupied with and fearful of their death. *Love of the dead* also implies love of material objects and other things, since the love of *things* is to love something which is *dead.*

Fromm's insights are valuable, and *To Have Or To Be?* is certainly worthwhile reading. He amplifies quite clearly how egoism and greed go hand in hand, both handmaidens to the having mode. In his view, egoism implies "wanting everything for myself," that "possessing, not sharing, gives me pleasure." A key theme of Fromm's book is referred to as "The End of An Illusion," this being "The Great Promise of Unlimited Progress," where promise and progress implies "the promise of domination of nature, of material abundance, of the greatest happiness for the greatest number, and of unimpeded freedom." The illusion also carries with it a false sense of omnipotence and omniscience: "We were on our way to becoming gods, supreme beings who could create a second world, using the natural world as building blocks for our new creation." He further notes that many of us are beginning to awaken from this illusion as we slowly and painfully begin to realize that unrestricted satisfaction of desires is not necessarily conducive to *well-being*, that the dream of being totally independent masters of our lives has turned us into "cogs in the bureaucratic machine," that economic progress has remained restricted to rich nations, at the expense of the poor, and that technological progress, unrestrained, has led to ecological danger, the danger of nuclear war, and the possibility of annihilation of all life itself.[7]

When Albert Schweitzer came to Oslo to accept the Nobel Prize for Peace, he addressed the world with the words "Man has become a superman. . . . But the superman with the superhuman power has not risen to the level of superhuman reason. . . . It must shake up our conscience that we become all the more inhuman the more we grow into supermen."

But does it shake up our conscience? Schweitzer spoke these words in 1952. In a way, his speech has, decades later, been proven true. Our lack of superhuman reason (or is it merely that we only need *human reason,* while presently using only *subhuman reason*?) has only persuaded us to race ahead in the fast lane—a race that unfortunately, if not further checked, may best be seen as a race to premature death. Is it really worth dying for?

NOTES

1   Breo, Dennis L., "Is It Worth Dying For?" *American Medical News,* May 15, 1981, p. 17.

2   Jenkins, C. D., "Psychological and Social Precursors of Coronary Disease," *The New England Journal of Medicine,* 84: 1971, pp. 244–55.

3   Friedman, Meyer, and Ray Rosenman, *Type A Behavior and Your Heart.* New York: Fawcett, 1974, p. 9.

4   *Ibid,* p. 14.

5   Slater, Philip, *Earthwalk.* New York: Bantam, 1974, p. 42.

6   Fromm, Erich, *To Have Or To Be?* New York: Bantam, 1976, p. 4.

7   *Ibid,* pp. xiii–xxiv.

chapter four

at whose expense?

God who has given us the love of women and the
friendship of men, keep alive in our hearts the
sense of old fellowship and tenderness; make
offenses to be forgotten and services remembered;
protect those whom we love in all things and
follow them with kindnesses, so that they may
lead simple and unsuffering lives, and in the
end die easily and with quiet minds.
—ROBERT LOUIS STEVENSON

Competition usually starts at a very young age, before youngsters are cognizant of what it actually is. Fathers sign their boys up for Little League, and, suddenly, what used to be a fun game becomes a life-and-death, matter-of-family-honor situation. Normally complacent daddies become wild-eyed, raging maniacs at the sidelines, urging Junior to "cream 'em," "slaughter the creep," and so on. Junior begins to realize that his best friend on the opposing team has become *The Enemy.* The sunny world of innocence has just ended. The competitive pressure is on—for life.

In Western culture—particularly here in the United

States—competition is an accepted way of life. It's apple pie, motherhood, and even baseball. It's ingrained in us from childhood, when we're taught to compete in school, sports, and even in friendship. Competition begets labeling: children become dumb or smart, athletic or clumsy, popular or antisocial. Later, competition lands us in "good" or "mediocre" colleges.

Down the road in the business world, workers compete against each other for jobs, promotions, and raises. Companies compete for customers, and advertising wars make the public aware of this competitive drive. Pepsi challenges RC and Coke in taste wars. Companies, whose products exhibit no real differences in ingredients or performance, go to wild extremes to let customers know that their aspirin, mineral water, gasoline, deodorants, and suppositories are "better." In turn, the customers ape this image-mania, and compete with one another by purchasing only the "better" brands.

Competition is not only a national propensity, but it has also managed to cross the language barrier as well. Japan competes with Detroit in automotive sales, Mexico goes at it with the Saudis for their share of petrodollars, and so forth. In addition to consumer goods, countries and governments compete against one another for territories and people. The propaganda is rife for capitalism versus communism, democracy versus socialism. But in spite of what our political leaders try to get us to believe, it's all merely a coverup for power lust. Self-interest is the true motive.

This competitiveness that we've had drilled into us from childhood leads us almost unknowingly into standard forms of daily behavior, that, if you stop to think about them, are actually quite bizarre. A husband may unconsciously encourage his wife to eat more or wear less makeup so that other men won't compete with him for her. A man who publicly praises a bright co-worker in his department may find this a dangerous practice, as that employee may just be the one to get the promotion he covets. A woman may subtly degrade her best friend's boyfriend because she is actually interested in him.

The variations go on and on. Husbands compete with wives (especially now that more women are in the job market), mothers compete with daughters, brothers compete with sisters, friends compete with friends. Our compulsion to compete has permeated every level and area of our social relationships.

Okay, a little competition and rugged individualism goes a long way. Without it, we may never have had pulsating shower massages, drive-through liquor stores, Godiva chocolates, and other creature comforts. On the other hand, too much *is* too much. We could certainly do without the nuclear arms race, oil embargos, and cola wars.

Non-stop competitiveness can be extremely damaging, both in personal and business life. It means that if someone has to win, someone else has to lose. For every success, there's usually a dismal failure. We focus all of our attention on the winners and reward them with love, money, trophies, Rolex watches and Blackglama minks. To the losers: nothing. We try to forget them as quickly as possible or until they turn around and become winners. But then there are the losers who don't turn around. The mentally ill, the poor, criminals and inmates, the handicapped, the addicts, and the "outcasts" are pushed aside while the rest of us chase after the brass ring.

How did this obsession with competition begin? Some say it's human instinct. Maybe cavemen tried to impress cavewomen by slaying the biggest woolly mammoth. No one is really sure. However, the competitive drive did seem to gain impetus with the dawn of Darwin in the mid-nineteenth century. *Social Darwinism* and the survival of the fittest flitted into our culture without question.

Another Western proclivity that has allowed competition to flourish relates to our ingrained ability to think only in binary units. The *either-or* mentality. You either get the job or you don't. You either succeed at your career or you don't. You'll either be rich or poor. Win-lose, me-you, do or die; we are thrown into a complete frenzy if a third option rears its confusing head. We are programmed for duality.

The quest for achievement and the thrill of success have reached epidemic proportions. Witness the number of books that have come out in the last decade stressing success and competition. Books like *Looking Out for Number 1*, *Mental Judo*, *Dressing For Success*, and *Only S.O.B.'s Succeed In Business* have become bestsellers. People really believe that in order to get ahead, they must resort to power plays, intimidation strategies, clout, maiming, and the like. The authors of these books become successful themselves simply by the amount of media exposure and royalties they receive. Few readers, if any, question their message or ethic.

But is there anything questionable about all of this? We say yes. For every winner there is bound to be a loser. Those who lose again and again are scathed; they will very likely develop personal problems (no one can remain optimistic if they're overlooked for a promotion for ten years) and maybe even mental illness. The number of corporate refugees whose permanent address is a psychiatric hospital is not small. Other losers turn to drugs and/or alcohol. Still others (and as far-fetched as this may seem to those of us who sit smugly in our three-piece-suited splendor in our executive offices) may turn to crime as an indirect way of getting back at society.

We all get caught up in the win/lose mentality to some degree at one time or another. Nobody wins all of the time. Yet when we lose—when we don't get that big account for the company—we can get resentful, anxious, frustrated, depressed, inadequate, and even paranoid. In other words, we feel stressed.

What do we do when we get this way? Assuming you

29

haven't yet been driven to robbing banks or checking into the Happy Valley Farm, you can start by questioning the assumption that all that competition is healthy. What are our alternatives? Well, the logical antidote to competition is cooperation. However, even this gets misused, as many people who subscribe to competition use cooperation as just another strategy: their real motive is winning. In addition, cooperation, the opposite of competition, is actually an either/or solution, perpetuating our binary, rigid thinking.

As we have previously mentioned in this book, one key to overcoming a conditioned obsession is to go beyond, to overcome our own base qualities. We can learn to think in a new way. We can start by training ourselves to forget our selfish, smaller selves and consider others—particularly Significant Others—like our employers, employees, friends, relatives, and lovers. What can we do that will be of interest to those *others*? Consider altruism—real altruism, not that phony stuff that gets us peer approval and VIP banquets in our honor. How about a little Anonymous Altruism where no one had to get the credit? We really have to relearn thinking and wishing the best for those around us. Let's not get obsessive about this either. But what if whole nations adopted this kind of new thinking? What kind of a world could it be?

Competition is also built upon making comparisons. Is my designer suit nicer than his? Is my automobile more expensive than hers? Are our kids smarter than theirs? The more competitive a person is, the more life becomes a nasty habit of comparison. At its farthest extremes, some way-out competitors make life a big game of one-upmanship. "He's got the Mercedes, that means I have to drive a Rolls Royce . . ." And paranoia and suspicion follow closely behind.

Though some may think that comparison-and-competition is the lifeblood of our society, it's healthy, at times, to step back and to become inner-directed rather than letting the masses mold you. How does one drop out of the rat race and become inner-directed? Here are some steps to get you started:

—Question assumptions, conditioning, values, interests, and opinions. Just because some of your friends say that they don't like foreign films (or traveling in Mexico, or blacks, or anything else), don't stay away from those movies because of their stated preferences. Find out for yourself. Explore. Investigate.

—Challenge authority, including that which emanates from politicians, experts, news people, teachers, and so on. A professor may have taught a subject for 43 years, but he may have taught it incorrectly for all those semesters. An economist may predict a recession when we're actually heading for a boom. Nobody is ever *always* right. Pointed questions keep people on their toes.

—Challenge dogma, theories, facts. What's true today—particularly in the rapidly changing fields of science—may be totally false tomorrow. Remember leeches and blood-letting? Those practices were part of "proven" medical facts not long ago. Even Margaret Mead has been given a run for her money in recent years.

—Learn to know yourself and to be honest with yourself. Do you want a managerial position only because everyone else wants one? Or could you find true happiness with a bit less responsibility, team-working with others? Don't let others decide what's best for you.

—Become independent and do things for yourself. Again, once you start relying on others, they may soon be deciding what's best for you. We're not advocating a hermit's life, but a key to healthy survival is the knowledge that you can do things for yourself, be it changing a light bulb or changing your job.

—Don't imitate others or conform to social pressures. If you're more comfortable putting Monets on your walls rather than Picassos, do it. If you really don't care about foreign sports cars, don't buy one.

—Learn to use your intuition and feelings. Though some may dismiss these less-logical aspects of human reasoning, they are very valuable. A gut-level reaction is almost always right. If you become nervous thinking about taking a job with a new company, don't do it. Those little voices in your head are worth listening to.

—Develop your own style. Don't be someone's shadow. Set your own standards. Be true to your own self.

chapter five

good humor

*It is impossible to experience
one's own death objectively
and still carry a tune.*
—WOODY ALLEN

Life these days doesn't seem all that funny. Let's see . . .
there's unemployment, nuclear proliferation, high interest
rates, and the Mid-East situation, and hemorrhoid preparations are being brazenly broadcast on television while most
Americans are sitting down to dinner. No, not much to
laugh about. Things are grim all over. Admittedly, it is
tough to chortle when filling up your gas tank requires you
to take out a second mortgage on your home or when you
discover you can't afford to buy a home at all.

But humor, laughter, and wit are essential to a healthy
and spiritual life, and given our general trends in society
today, they are qualities that are becoming rarer. When was
the last time you giggled, laughed, snickered, or fell apart
for more than 30 seconds? Chances are if you did, someone
might have tried to slap and subdue you, thinking you had
leaped off the deep end.

For many, chortling may not seem to be the best route

to higher consciousness, but when you stop to think about it, humor and spirituality *are* linked. According to Arthur Koestler, "The psychology of the creative process is, oddly enough, most clearly revealed in humor and wit." By allowing humor into your life, you are opening up your mind to learning. Humor outwits the conditioned mind; it forces us to think—to contemplate. It can be used to display and reveal the foibles of human behavior.

With humor—therefore allowing yourself to be creative—you can ready your mind for higher, unfamiliar experiences, such as enlightenment. In fact, the Sufis and Zen Buddhists regularly utilize humor in their teaching tales. Advanced spiritual sages are frequently referred to as "wise fools" because they are seemingly possessed by a form of divine zaniness. But they know something we should all be aware of: laughter is life-enhancing, positive, and leads to perception.

With all its wonderful qualities, what has driven the giggles out of us? Current events, surely. Dourness has become a normal state for most of us, especially after we read the newspaper. But this natural mourning seems to have its roots much deeper in our psyches. There are theories that this lack of laughter goes back to the beginnings of Judeo-Christian cultures.

In his book, *You Shall Be As Gods*, Erich Fromm notes that, whereas the origins of the Judeo-Christian tradition were intended to be of an uplifting nature—that is, they were meant to serve as an inspiration to humanity to strive from beast to human, suffering to joy—in the past two millennia the original intent of religion and the Scriptures has dissipated or has become misconstrued. The beast has persisted, and the suffering has endured. The problem seems to have begun with the Crucifixion. Fromm notes that many scholars and theologians have interpreted the Crucifixion as depicting Christ in despair. This may be, as Fromm notes, because Christ died reciting Psalm 22, a

Psalm commonly thought to be despairing in content. But, as Fromm reveals quite clearly in his book, while the Psalm begins in despair, the key phrase (Verse 21), "Thou hast answered me," implies that despair has been transformed into hope and faith, and that the Crucifixion, if anything, should have led to confidence instead of despair. Fromm also notes that, "The last stanza . . . consists of five verses and no longer contains even the memory of despair. It expresses unmitigated hope, faith and enthusiasm, and ends with another 'perfect'—the certainty *ki-asah*, 'he has wrought it.' The last verses are said in a mood of enthusiasm and of messianic hope for the deliverance of all mankind."[1]

We're not saying that the Crucifixion should be the subject of a comedy film (although the comedy troupe, Monty Python, did do a wickedly funny movie a few years back based on the beginnings of Christianity). However, the Crucifixion has become more of a disaster because of humanity's reaction to it (or misinterpretation of it) than the occurrence itself. The obsession with Christ's death has obscured the original intention of Christianity itself.

> *The Crucifixion was a disaster because it established attitudes which were quite contrary to Christianity itself and have cramped Christianity ever since. Christianity opened up man's attitudes to his fellow men in terms of love and tolerance. The Crucifixion, however, emphasized the sharp polarization of good and evil that put all the intolerance into the practical administration of Christianity. The Crucifixion made fear, sin, and guilt the motive force. It also bred the arrogance, righteousness, and dogmatism that are the other side of the polarization. The world might have been a better place if somehow the Crucifixion had simply been dropped out of Christian teaching, because once it was there it was so powerful that it had to become the central point. It would then have been necessary to demonstrate divine love by living example rather than by reference to an historic death. It is interesting that religions like Islam and Buddhism which have no equivalent to the Crucifixion have always been more tolerant.*[2]

In his book, *The Happiness Purpose,* **Dr.** Edward de-Bono notes that religion has taught people to be stoic, to endure (and almost pursue) suffering. Religion has become typically based on sin: anything pleasurable, it seems, from overindulging in brownies to having sex more than once a week, swiftly succumbs to the slime of sin. As a result, religion has become overly associated with solemnity and self-abdication. Today, we're just one step ahead of the self-flagellators of yore. Religion has also become synonymous with fear, shame, and guilt—all negative emotions, even though Woody Allen has elevated them to superstar status. This triad of bad vibes can ultimately lead to depression, one of the most uncomfortable and disabling chronic conditions of all.

Most of us are all too familiar with the numerous prune-faced religionists (note: we are not saying *all* of them, just a lot) of all persuasions who see no place for humor in religion. When was the last time you saw a preacher do a stand-up routine in the pulpit á la Rodney Dangerfield? To many of them, a good one-liner is blasphemy. And, as they thunder out over their congregations, they obviously convince their followers as well.

The idea that religion is about as funny as a flat tire in the middle of the Mojave Desert in July is something alien to those who actually founded religions. Jesus, for example, who was fond of children, is on record as having declared, "Unless you turn and become like children you will never enter the Kingdom of Heaven" (Matthew 18:3). Mohammed was well-known for his sense of humor, and one of the Prophet's companions, Abdulla, son of Harith, stated, "I have never seen anyone who smiled more than the Messenger of Allah." And, of course, those familiar with Zen Buddhism will recognize the "smile of truth," the "laughing monks," and the "smiling Buddha." And Buddha himself is credited by the sutras as having smiled on numerous occasions, these situations typically associated with enlightenment—the sight of sublime truth—or upon registering the

36

ludicrousness of the unenlightened. Undoubtedly, Buddha would have smiled at the deadpan, obsessive cleric of today.

Perhaps then, for our own personal growth, it's time to get back to the roots of religion. In his classic book *The Psychology of Laughter and Comedy*, J. Y. T. Greig makes an excellent case for the hypothesis, ". . . that laughter, in its beginnings at least, is somehow associated with the instinct of love."[3] This instinct of love is something we are all born with; we come into this world as infants with a broad spectrum of positive qualities and inclinations. And we keep them until religion, family, culture, and everything else drum us into grim submission. Greig reveals how this instinct of love contains many psychoemotional behaviors in infants and young children we would normally associate with humor and laughter: smiling, ticklishness, romping about, glee, delight, friendly teasing, and play. In other words, laughter—humor—is a natural state. To be perma-depressed is not.

Certainly, feeling secure and loved is conducive to merriment and laughter. On the other hand, feeling insecure or anxious, uncertain of oneself, unloved or incapable of giving love—being neurotic—is conducive to the inability to laugh (interestingly, Woody Allen, America's number-one neurotic, has made others laugh at his inabilities). A well-balanced person is, among other things, distinguished by his or her quality of being fun-loving and fun-experiencing. Most neurotics may best be described as *fun-deficient*—they are often quite bored (and boring as well). One psychoanalyst, Dr. Edward Bergler, made an insightful observation when he noted that "Boredom represents an unconscious defense mechanism created by the unconscious ego under pressure of a frantic superego attack. *It is a preventive method of proving I'm a good boy. The method consists of clearing all dangerous and incriminating material out of the psychic chambers, leaving them empty.*"[4]

Not only is fun-deficiency related to neuroticism or mental illness, but recently it's also been linked to physical

37

illnesses. Raymond Moody, M.D., provides numerous examples of uptight and rigid patients, who were chronically ill, in his book *Laugh After Laugh*. We've all known John and Jane Does who gave themselves ulcers and cancers by living life in the no-passing lane. In many cases, the illness could have been averted had the patient learned to lighten up, get down, and get funky. Dr. Moody also notes that a major threat to the health of patients across the world can often be a brusque, rigid doctor with the bedside manner of a postal clerk.

The role of laughter in healthy functioning is best documented in Norman Cousins' top seller, *Anatomy of an Illness,* wherein Cousins relates how a steady regimen of laughter (along with an improved nutritional intake) cured him of a "terminal" disease. Cousins, apparently unable to find much humor in his ordinary life, was able to inject laughter into his life by spending several hours each day watching the popular TV show Candid Camera and old Marx Brothers movies. Reading joke books also helped.

All of which probably makes us wonder what makes us laugh and more important why we laugh. In her master's thesis at the University of Chicago (1965) entitled "A Study of Humor in Children's Books," Katherine Hull Kappas arrived at ten separate categories of what makes not only children, but adults as well, laugh. Her classifications include exaggeration (ladies, gentlemen and Joan Rivers . . .), incongruity (. . . "Sock it to *me?*" asked a bewildered Richard M. Nixon of yore), surprise (something Ricky always seemed to register when he came home to his beloved Lucy), slapstick (Moe, Larry, and Curly), the absurd (Steve Martin), human predicaments (Charlie Chaplin's forté), ridicule (Abbot and Costello, Laurel and Hardy), defiance (Don Rickles), verbal humor (oh, for the Dorothy Parker days . . .), and violence (especially if it's out of context). There. Is that ten?

Finding out why we laugh isn't nearly as cut-and-dry as figuring out what makes us laugh. Numerous theories abound. In his book, *Laughter and the Sense of Humor*, Edmund Bergler lists over 70 different theories of laughter, including those of Plato, Aristotle, Cicero, Hobbes, Descartes, Locke, Spinoza, Kant, Goethe, Freud, and others. Theorists have proposed that we laugh for all kind of reasons, such as relief, as a way to disguise aggression (as in ridicule), as escape from depression, as an expression of sudden joy, and so on. Bergler notes that with the preponderance of diverse theories of laughter, disagreement abounds. Being a psychoanalyst, he favors Freud's theories on wit and humor and discusses further elaborations.

Because his book was written in 1956, Bergler was not familiar with Arthur Koestler's superb analyses of humor, expounded in his classic work, *The Act of Creation* (1964). Koestler reveals how comedy (wit and humor) is essentially an act of creativity, with "insight" as its essence (the "ha! ha!" and "a! ha!" reflexes essentially related). Both comedy (or wit) and insight being creative, Koestler views the *art of creation* as an association of two or more thought matrices—frames of reference—that were previously unconnected with one another. Edward deBono holds a similar view, relating humor to insight:

> *In humor there is a switch-over from the obvious way of looking at things to another way which is just as plausible. We can see that the new way is possible, but it really is not very likely. So from a practical point of view, humor is not very constructive, though it can still be useful in easing rigid views and fierce situations. Insight is exactly the same process as humor, but with insight, the switch-over is to a new way of looking at things that is much better than the original way.* [5]

DeBono explains that the human brain/mind functions by setting up and preserving familiar patterns of thought. "Humor involves switching out of the obvious pattern to use a different one." The essence of a brain/mind pattern is that it is "established and therefore predictable."

Patterns set up expectation(s), and when the expectation is foiled, humor may result. He gives the following as an example, titled "Two Politicians":

> *At dinner one evening Winston Churchill was placed next to Lady Astor, who was known for her forthright views. She was angry with Mr. Churchill, and turning to him, she said, "Mr. Churchill, if I were married to you I should put poison in your coffee." The expectation is that Mr. Churchill would resent having poison put in his coffee and would therefore counter with some awful vengeance of his own. But his reply was, "Madam, if I were married to you, I should drink that coffee."*[6]

In another book, *The Happiness Purpose,* Dr. deBono asserts, "It has always surprised me how little attention philosophers have paid to humor since it is a more important process of mind than is reason." DeBono justifies his position with sound discussion, concluding with the further assertion that humor can be a valuable attitude towards life itself, and a key process in perception. He sees humor as positive and life-enhancing: "The purpose of humor is enjoyment and happiness." Humor is "anti-solemnity" and "anti-arrogance." "Humor is for tolerance and humility." In the process of perception, humor ". . . allows the mind to switch over and *look at something in a completely new way.*"[7]

Of course, deBono notes that the positive aspects of humor can be overdone. If you spend most of your day laughing, people around you may have you quietly committed to the Happy Valley Farm for the Existentially Distorted. DeBono does not suggest that we become perpetually obnoxious, back-slapping buffoons. The full-time twits and practical jokers are unknowing cranks. He also underscores the negative aspects of humor, the cynicism and sarcasm, which, unchecked, could become the weed that chokes out the Bermuda grass of life. Too much laughing or sneering at everything implies ". . . that nothing is ever worth doing and the only solution is to drift along without

40

effort or activity." But de Bono recognizes that this exploitation of humor is the sign of a more deeply rooted negative attitude towards life, which is really the opposite of the intention of humor: "The sneer is false humor. The true attitude is the deliberate putting on of fancy dress and enjoying it, knowing that it may be ridiculous if you choose to regard it as such—but not minding."[8]

So humor can be an essential component of a happy, healthy life. Without it, we would be walking in a Calvinist cloud. Humor can also open our eyes to new possibilities.

It was philosopher Søren Kierkegaard who once said, "When I was young I forgot to laugh. Later, when I opened my eyes and saw reality . . . I began to laugh and haven't stopped since." The idea of "seeing reality"—spiritual awakening—is often associated in spiritual literature with laughter and joy. In Eastern psychospiritual religions, this idea is sometimes referred to as getting "the cosmic joke." In Sufi psychospiritual training, the "joke-tale" is considered an essential part of the learning process. The Mulla Nasrudin tales are well-known the world over. Nasrudin, the everyman of the Arab world, is at once both wiseman and fool. While he always evokes laughter, closer notice reveals something of value for all of us. His stories typically illustrate the antics of the human mind—our penchant for self-deception, our use of defense mechanisms, and our overreliance upon logic. Study of the Nasrudin tales assists one in the development of intuition and perception.

> The Mulla was acting tired.
> "Go buy some meat for tonight's dinner," said his wife.
> "Too tired," replied the Mulla.
> Later on, "Get some firewood."
> "I'm tired," groaned the Mulla.
> Later, "Get the fire going."
> "How many times must I remind you—I'm tired."
> Then the dinner was cooked and ready.
> "As tired as I am, I don't have the nerve to refuse you any longer," said the Mulla as he headed for the bowl of food.

41

It may well be that people who have lost their sense of humor, who can no longer have an honest laugh, while clinically alive, are spiritually dead—they have no soul. This concords with the words of Sigmund Freud where he states that humor is ". . . one of the highest psychic functions, enjoying the special favor of thinkers." So perhaps we should heed the advice of those three words the fashionable people are wearing as 14-karat charms around their necks: "Live, love, (and most important) laugh." The rest will come more easily.

NOTES

1   Fromm, Erich, *You Shall Be As Gods*. New York: Fawcett, 1966, p. 173.
2   DeBono, Edward, *Po: Beyond Yes and No*. New York: Penguin, 1973, pp. 28–29.
3   Greig, J. Y. T., *The Psychology of Laughter and Comedy*. New York: Cooper Square, 1969, p. 44.
4   Bergler, Edward, *Laughter and the Sense of Humor*. New York: Intercontinental Medical Books, 1956, pp. 217–218.
5   DeBono, *op. cit.*, p. 83.
6   *Ibid*, p. 81.
7   DeBono, Edward, *The Happiness Purpose*. New York: Penguin, 1977, p. 81.
8   *Ibid*, p. 82.

chapter six

spirituality
in action

*There is a time in every man's education when he
arrives at the conviction that envy is ignorance;
that imitation is suicide; that he must take himself
for better, for worse, as his portion; that though
the wide universe is full of good, no kernal
of nourishing corn can come to him but through
his toil bestowed on that plot of ground which is
given to him to till.*
—RALPH WALDO EMERSON

Harry is, well, rather chubby, and he's been that way most of
his life. Yet he's always "on a diet" and knows more about
calories and carbohydrates than he does about his wife's
personality. Henry talks about diets while he eats Snickers.
All talk—no action.

Deborah joins every committee in town and volunteers
for every task. She lets everyone know how she will tackle a
certain project and how wonderful it will be under her
guidance. But when it comes down to actual work, Deborah
always seems to be missing in action and has a hundred
good excuses as to why she wasn't able to do the job. All
talk—no action.

Like dieting, completing projects, making money, and helping others, spirituality doesn't happen if you just talk about it. It has to be translated into deeds. In order to lead a better, more spiritual life, you must simply *do* it.

The first step to taking action toward a spiritual life is to *awaken* or become aware. Not that we lead horrible, criminal lives, but most of the time we don't really think about what we do or why. We lead our lives (or they lead us) on automatic pilot.

In the April 1982 issue of *Psychology Today,* in an article entitled "Automated Lives," psychologist Ellen J. Langer discusses her research on what she describes as "mindlessness." In numerous experiments, she discovered that most people exhibit mindlessness: "a condition in which people unwittingly respond to the world as if they were automatons . . . a state of reduced cognitive activity." She gives an example of an experiment in which people were much more willing to give up their place in line at a Xerox machine to someone else who gives them a reason, even if the reason ("I have to make some copies") is redundant. Langer contrasts mindlessness with something quite its opposite, "mindfulness." She finds mindfulness to be much less common than mindlessness but believes that conscientious people can develop it even though it might require special ongoing and creative efforts. In summarizing her research, Langer states,

> Taken as a whole, then, the mindless/mindful distinction is . . . relevant for understanding individual behavior, interpersonal relations, feelings of mastery, physical health, successful aging, and possibly longevity. Thus, it is clear that even though there is no way that one can consider everything in the environment mindfully, it is to everyone's advantage always to be mindfully considering something.[1]

It has been stated more than once by ancients as well as some modern-day psychologists that we tend to exist in a

44

state of sleep (mindlessness?) and that one primary objective of spiritual effort is to awaken (mindfulness). When we speak of spirituality, we are indeed speaking of effort and action. Spirituality is not an abstraction or philosophical concept. It is an activity.

As a beautiful flower that is full of hue but lacks fragrance, even so fruitless is the well-spoken word of one who does not practice it.

—BUDDHA

Thus, in order to progress on the road to spirituality, we must first awaken and then take action. Spirituality in action does not have to take place in a cathedral or in a barren cave in India. Spirituality can be applied directly to your everyday life; you can be truly human with your Aunt Martha, with the person who signs your paychecks, and in the way you relate to strangers.

Let's see how you can put spirituality in action in three basic areas of your life: vocation, interactions with others, and ethical behavior.

CHOICE OF VOCATION. Steve was a Wall Street stockbroker. He was quite successful, made decent money, and diligently commuted to work. But he hated it. One day he packed his bags and traded the canyons of New York for the Grand Canyon State. He decided to pursue his true loves—art and photography—by opening an art gallery. Today, he's happy and successful—both financially and emotionally.

Steve, like many other people today, put *his* spirituality into action by choosing to pursue a vocation that fulfilled him, not a vocation that simply earned him dollars. Because he is happy and truly interested in his work, he can do his best for others—his happiness has a ripple effect. Your vocation choice need not be dictated by money and training alone. Your work must be meaningful to both yourself and society.

45

On the other hand, pursuing your "true" vocation doesn't necessarily mean giving up your credit cards. A job should not just be good for your soul. It should be right for your checking account as well. Giving up a successful law practice to raise organic cucumbers for $3000 a year plus salad will simply take the meat and potatoes off the table.

Interestingly, there is a new movement afoot called "right livelihood." It involves making a conscious choice about your employment situation. With the right livelihood, you work at a particular job because you *want* to be there and/or your work makes a positive, constructive contribution to society. It's not healthy to be involved in a career or a job just because you spent four years studying the subject in college, your parents did the same work, or it's easy money. If you are doing something of value, if your heart is in it, you can do any kind of work.

With the right livelihood, you make a life, not a living. Money means nothing if you have to sell your soul or be bored to get it. Having private time, working in a pleasant environment, and being with positive, creative people all contribute to the right livelihood. If you are not happy with your life, consider changing your work, or going out on your own.

Here are some specific questions to ask yourself. You may find out whether or not you're in the right job, spiritually.

—Does your work allow you to grow and evolve?

—Are you learning something *daily* (no matter how little)?

—Are you content, happy, stimulated?

—Are you of service to others?

—Does your work contribute in some way to the betterment (as opposed to harm) of the world?

INTERACTION WITH OTHERS. Alvin owned a small retail business that was fairly successful. He ran his business with an iron fist. Employees worked six days a week with no over-time compensation. He frowned when they laughed or when they appeared to have a good time in the store. Alvin often accused them of taking change from the cash register. If he had to be out of town, he hired a private detective to hang around the store to keep an eye on his people. Nobody got raises there, nor were they allowed a day off for sickness or personal emergencies. Vacations? Alvin was the only one allowed to take them.

He often wondered why he could never keep a sales-person longer than six months and why his former employees never spoke to him when he ran into them. If Alvin were drowning, it's doubtful that one of his employ-ees would come to his rescue.

Alvin's problem: his interaction with others. Not that he *didn't* interact with people; his interactions were negative and tinged with anger, hatred, paranoia, and mistrust. And as the saying goes, what goes around comes around. The reaction to his style of interaction is decidedly negative.

How a person interacts with others—be it bosses, em-ployees, cousin Harold, the neighbors, the clerk at the con-venience store—is definitely a step toward (or away from) spirituality. These days, it's not easy to stay on the right, positive track toward this goal. On one hand, we were raised with "do unto others" whispered gently in our little ears. Now, books like *Power!*, *Winning Through Intimidation,* and others shriek at you to stop being a wide-eyed Pollyana and forge ahead for yourself.

That's it. Intimidate your neighbor into loaning you his hedge clipper. Muscle your way into running a business and take credit for everything. Demand that your spouse make love to you 5.2 nights of the week. Now, does anybody like you?

Sure, everyone wants to be successful at whatever they do, but does one have to get there by being cruel to others or by intimidating people? Winning skirmishes through these techniques provides for only temporary wins. Real success comes through positive spiritual interactions with others.

47

You should always realize that the other person should also benefit from an interaction.

Whatever you do, it always reflects on you.

ETHICS. An article in the November-December, 1981, issue of *Harvard Business Review,* entitled "Ethics Without the Sermon," by Laura L. Nash, an assistant professor of business administration at the Harvard Business School, posits that corporate executives will only take a close look at the matter of ethics when it affects the profit picture. Thus, according to her, the movers and shakers of the business world will only consider ethical issues under conditions where, for example, they may be facing a hefty and well-publicized lawsuit related to liability or discrimination (remember Ford's Pinto?). Or, ethics could be used as a public relations gesture, thereby increasing long-term profits.

Nash goes on to note that the corporate ethos concerning ethics is ultimately subservient to profits. She concludes that "the good corporation is expected to avoid perpetuating irretrievable social injury (and to assume the costs when it unintentionally does injury), while focusing on its purposes as a profit-making organization. Its moral capacity does not extend, however, to determining by itself what will improve the general social welfare."[4]

If this is Nash's view of corporate ethics, what's her definition of *unethical?* Unfortunately, there seem to be a lot of people who may agree with her. The goal of bigger and bigger profits has become the ethic. "Ethics" is now being defined as "that which suits us," a bastardization of the true spirit of ethics. The spirit of real ethics can be brought into viable practice in the business (and personal) world of the 1980s. Ethics can be reintroduced without the sermon, but determining what will improve the general social welfare *is* everyone's responsibility. Until we recognize this, all of us stand to lose out, including the corporate executives who live among us.

We are entering into a new era of human awareness—one of rethinking and reevaluating. What was, does not necessarily have to be. It's an era in which the climate is becoming more receptive to basic ethical considerations and, yes, the general social welfare. The *winning-at-any-cost* syndrome is (thankfully) headed for the wastebasket.

Think about ethics in your daily life. Without realizing it, you probably make a dozen or so ethical decisions throughout the course of a typical day. When you leave for work in the morning do you purposely neglect to tell your spouse that you are having lunch with a very attractive member of the opposite sex? If you're invited to dinner with a group of friends and you just don't feel like going, do you fib and say you have a blinding headache, or do you go? Do you start padding your expense account just a tiny bit when you find out that your raise isn't quite as hefty as you thought it would be? Ethics surround us at all times. The decisions you make rely on your own moral makeup.

This is a time when, both on a business and personal level, we are beginning to look within, to look at the *quality* of our lives, rather than merely being obsessed with external, materialistic concerns. Two BMW's in every garage, designer labels affixed to every end of our bodies, and the latest in microwave ovens cannot conceal our real poverties in life. We are now looking at our state of *wellness,* at the quality of our relationships, and at our need to feel good, happy, and fulfilled. A sense of emptiness cannot be obliterated by the amount of consumer goods purchased on one shopping spree. The vacuum can only be satisfied by an enrichment of our experiences, our personal psychology, and our peace of mind.

There's no doubt that over the past hundred years or so there has been a marked absence of a workable personal and social ethic. Our most gloriously demeaning qualities—greed, self-interest, vanity, loss of compassion—

have run rampant. Symptoms abound: mental illness, stress, "burn-out," alcoholism, drug abuse, crime, pollution, war, and disillusionment.

But does it have to be this way? Has our worst side finally gotten the best of us? Probably not. And that's not being optimistic. The latest research in personal and social psychology reveals that our current state of individual and social life is far from the "norm." By norm, we refer to basic, healthy human nature, not to statistical averages. The problem does not appear to lie totally within human nature, but within our culture—our shared beliefs, habits, attributes, values, and practices. In other words, our lack of a viable ethic.

A government-sponsored study further drives the point home. The study, under the direction of Marian Radke Yarrow, chief of the Laboratory of Developmental Psychology at the National Institute of Mental Health, revealed that babies are born with an inherent sense of ethics, that they have "amazingly generous impulses" and "perform acts of altruism at a surprisingly early age." The children, who were between the ages of 10 months and 2½ years, had a capacity for compassion and exhibited various kinds of prosocial behavior from as early as the age of one. Interestingly, it is quite easy for us to believe that such characteristics are not a part of our basic nature because most parents view this type of behavior as weak and, therefore, undesirable, so it is subtly discouraged. According to Yarrow, "People have little use for altruism in this society, except when it's institutionalized, as through charities and volunteer services." Charity has become a conditioned public virtue. So the major culprit appears to be our culture.

We verify this by examining the subtleties of other cultures. To Hopi Indians, being helpful to others is a primary social practice. To have a "Hopi good heart" is second nature and does not require extra effort. On the other hand, there are cultures like the Ik of Uganda, whose sense of self-interest is even more highly developed (so to

50

speak) than our own. Little, if any, compassion is ever demonstrated, not even for children or parents. To feed oneself and to satisfy personal needs is the only motivator with the Ik.

Our inherent human nature is basically ethical and healthy. Not only do we have an underlying conscience, but additional psychological research has also discovered that human potentials are infinite, as is human adaptability. As Claude M. Steiner has noted in his book, *Scripts People Live,* "Intimacy, awareness, and spontaneity are innately human and, even if crushed, will reemerge again and again with each succeeding generation."

We all need to dig deeply and rediscover our ethical and moral selves. This discovery will contribute to the betterment of us all. It's practical, expedient, and healthy. Ethics, when carried out beyond the fluorescently-lit confines of the office, can cure many of our personal and social ills. Practiced collectively on a wide scale, ethics may contribute to a sense of international brotherhood and world peace. Not practiced at all, we may become one large tribe of Ik.

In line with our return to the bosom of ethics, there is a movement stirring known as "voluntary simplicity," a lifestyle that avoids complexities and revolves around consideration for others, for your growth, and for the future of the world. It's an attitude and a new sense of values that carries ethics beyond decision-making stages and into action.

Take, for example, someone who has come into a bit of money or has earned it after much hard work. If voluntary simplicity is practiced, that money could be used to enhance and enrich one's inner self—education, travel, reading, exploring. The money would probably *not* be used to buy a large, gas-guzzling Statusmobile, a huge house that costs a lot of money to maintain, or faddy clothing that's out of style in two months. With voluntary simplicity, one consciously pares one's life down to only that which can be

51

treasured within one's self and that which may also have a positive effect upon society.

There are other everyday things you can do to practice voluntary simplicity (you don't have to give up everything). For one thing, you *can* fight our society's mass consumption mentality by recycling household items like newspapers and bottles and avoiding purchasing things that contribute to pollution. Simplify your food intake to only that which you need to keep you healthy and vital. Don't waste your money on soft drinks or over-salted snack foods that give you nothing, nutritionally. Walk or ride a bicycle when possible. Avoid work environments that cut your senses off from nature. Use solar energy, plant your own garden, rely less on others. Above all, don't get attached to "things."

Thus, it becomes obvious that lip-flapping about spirituality is meaningless. Spirituality must be transformed into action. It must be intertwined with your vocation, your dealings with others, your morality, and your lifestyle. Don't just say it. Do it.

NOTES

1   Langer, Ellen J., "Automated Lives." *Psychology Today*, April, 1982, p. 71.
2   Nash, Laura L., "Ethics Without the Sermon." *Harvard Business Review*, November-December, 1981, p. 89.

chapter seven

world as illusion

*If the doors of perception were cleansed every
thing would appear to man as it is, infinite.*

*For man has closed himself up, til he sees all
things thro' narrow chinks of his cavern.*

—WILLIAM BLAKE

You pay your dollars at the box office, buy the popcorn, and
wedge yourself into the theater's seats. The lights dim, the
crowd quiets down, and the credits begin. Within a few
minutes, you're lost in the plot. You stop noticing that the
popcorn tastes like mattress stuffing and that the man next
to you has rattling adenoids. Your world has become that of
the screen. When the leading man sweeps the love of his life
off her feet, *you are there.* For those 120 minutes or so, those
flickering frames are your reality.

What is reality? What is an illusion? Good questions.
Relatively speaking, reality seems to be whatever you *believe*
in, what you *create* for yourself, and—most important—that
which is reinforced by the elements in your world. While
you're in that theater, that's reality; and while you're shopping for silk shirts at I. Magnin, that's reality too. And

illusion, put simply, is the opposite of reality: that which is not real.

Let's delve into the rather elusive subject of reality a bit more. In an interesting study, psychologist Charles Tart trained two of his graduate assistants, a young man and woman, in a method of mutual hypnosis. First, Tart had the woman hypnotize the man, then, after he was hypnotized, the man was trained to hypnotize the woman. While maintaining rapport with both of them, Tart taught them techniques that would allow them to take each other deeper and deeper into the trance. Simply by chance, Tart discovered that these mutual techniques became a shared, conceptual reality for both of them. For example, the man instructed the woman to go deeper into hypnosis by imagining herself walking deeper and deeper into a tunnel. After she crept further into the tunnel, she would beckon the man to follow her. And naturally, after a few tunneling experiences, they actually found themselves in a tunnel. It took on full sensory reality. They could see it, feel its walls and its dampness, and hear their echoes. Eventually, they could not distinguish their "tunnel" reality from ordinary reality. They were *there*. Interestingly, Tart was able to convince a *third* subject to enter the couple's tunnel world.

Perhaps, then, things are the same to all, or most, of us in our "reality." Like the hypnosis subjects, we convince one another that, yes, we really are in a tunnel, a recession, a democracy, or whatever. We reinforce what is real (in other words, permissible by society) because we seem to want everyone to conform and we fear deviation.

Writer Joseph Chilton Pearce, in his book *Magical Child*, relates the story of a college student who was in the habit of indulging in LSD. While he and a mind-expansion-oriented friend were flying high, another friend dropped in on them. This particular friend apparently dabbled in nothing stronger than herbal tea. After trying to deal with the two trippers, the third friend became caught up in their multi-colored nirvana and tripped right along with them. Contact high, it's called. Their reality became his. They convinced one another that it was real.

But is ordinary life that real? Dr. Arthur Deikman, in his book, *The Observing Self,* notes that ". . . introspection demonstrates that much of the time we dwell on abstract, tangential thoughts and fantasies. When we suddenly shift from such preoccupations to a full, vivid awareness of the world, the contrast is so great we may describe ourselves as 'coming to' or 'waking up.' Correspondingly, someone deeply absorbed in thought and fantasies is said to be 'in a trance.' . . . The predilection of people to be preoccupied with imaginings to confine their attention to narrow segments of reality, is a tendency [which] . . . I call . . . the trance of ordinary life."[1]

Deikman has also discussed hypnosis, and notes that the hypnotic state is not dissimilar from ordinary consciousness. "So habitual is the trance of ordinary life that one could say that human beings are a race that sleeps and awakens, but does not awaken fully. Because half-awake is sufficient for the tasks we customarily do, few of us are aware of the dysfunction of our condition. Moments of more complete awakening do occur, but the consensus of the group . . . automatic functioning . . . make such phenomena transient curiosities rather than urgent signals that something is wrong with the normal state."[2]

The findings of Tart, Pearce, and Deikman should strike us as more than mere curiosity. It's quite easy for us to slip into another reality. Perhaps then, this is a signal that something's not quite right—not quite satisfying enough— in ordinary life.

Clearly, ordinary, day-to-day, pay-your-bills life is not the *only* reality. Again, our reality is predominantly that which society has programmed into us—that which is desirable or permissible. This programming also gives us the distinct impression that there can be no other forms of reality. Yet we slip into others easily. We live in the metaphorical tunnel. To lead fuller, richer lives, we must learn to acknowledge our tunnel, and then begin finding our way out. Consensual reality is not the only form of reality.

Possibly the best reference on the nature and dynamics of consensual reality is Charles Tart's book, *States of Consciousness*. He notes that the responsible agent for developing our consensual reality is culture, or more specifically, the enculturation process that begins in the cradle (or even in the womb) and ends in the grave:

> *A culture can be seen as a group which has selected certain human potentials as good and developed them, and rejected others as bad. Internally, this means that certain possible experiences are encouraged and others suppressed to construct a "normal" state of consciousness that is effective in and helps define the culture's particular consensus reality. The process of enculturation begins in infancy, and by middle childhood the individual has a basic membership in consensus reality. . . . By adulthood, the individual enjoys maximum benefits from membership, but he is now maximally bound. . . . A person's "simple" perception of the world and of others is actually a complex process controlled by many implicit factors.* [3]

As an example of this social conditioning we find ourselves taking part in, let's take a walk in a winter wonderland and examine snow. Snow is snow, right? That's what most of us are taught. But to an avid skier there are different types of snow, including powder, wet snow, and corn snow. A skier has been *encultured* to believe in those types of snow. Even more astounding, Eskimos are trained to distinguish at least seven types of snow. When your color spectrum consists of mostly white, you begin to see subtle variations.

Most of the controlling factors of enculturation are subtle or hidden—out of awareness. It is as if everyone in a given culture has been hypnotized. This is a form of "mutual hypnosis" in which each of us hypnotizes one another into believing, and then mutually perceiving, the same things. This process has many names, all implying the same thing: conditioning, brainwashing, indoctrination, programming.

Despite our abilities to invest money successfully into real estate, to apply nail polish without smudging it, and to resist a second helping of carrot cake, we have an innate "lemmingness" about us. We do have (despite our denials) a tendency toward conformity and suggestibility, and, like those rodents who follow each other into the sea, we easily fall into a sea of consensual reality. Not only do we all tend to generally *do* the same things, but we all tend to perceive and experience most of the same things.

Dr. Edward deBono, in his book *Mechanism of Mind*, illuminates how the development of consensual reality is facilitated by the structure and dynamics of the brain. The brain provides us with the ability to organize incoming sensory signals into meaningful patterns. Once the patterns become established, they become familiar, and once those patterns become familiar, it's exceedingly difficult to change them. It is hard to teach an old brain new tricks. Pretty soon that pattern becomes the exclusive way of thinking. Let's say that as a mere toddler, you learn to brush your teeth a certain way. The first few times, it's not that easy to handle that colored stick with the good-tasting cream on it. You want to play with it and then eat the toothpaste. But after awhile, the task loses its intrigue and becomes routine, familiar. Pretty soon, it's automatic. So, what happens when your dentist, some twenty or thirty years later, tells you to brush your teeth differently? It's almost impossible to do it. Your brain has pre-instructed your hands in the technique.

When interrelated patterns of thought or perception connect together into larger systems of patterns, it becomes what deBono calls *meta-systems* (brushing teeth is akin to oral hygiene, which is related to overall health, which is related to vitality, which is related to life and living, and on and on). To expand this a bit, deBono calls a consensually agreed upon reality within a given culture a *social meta-system*. And, as he notes, if this social meta-system gets its blessing from an even higher source, such as religion, almost nothing can disassemble it or even blast it apart. These meta-systems are so powerful (yet subtle and implicit) that they can efface all personal or social realities. DeBono illustrates this with the example of the Christian martyrs, singing to their deaths in the Colosseum of Rome. Because their belief was so strong, they were willing to sacrifice their lives. These Christians had their fatalistic beliefs conditioned into them by their culture and the religion of that culture.

So dying in the dirt with thousands of people watching was the martyrs' reality. It was also their illusion, their world. It was their *perception* of how things were. It was the result of conditioning, beliefs, values, and assumptions. Perception, it appears, can be a strange thing. It can twist things and make insignificant, trivial things seem important (or important things seem trivial). It can make the world an illusion.

Continuing with the world-as-illusion theme, a close relationship exists between cultural assumptions (or pre-conceptions) and illusion. Hence, in a society that believes in "evil spirits," its citizens utilize various techniques or behaviors to ward them off. When someone dies or some catastrophe occurs, these beliefs of evil spirits become enhanced.

> *Similarly, in a society where war is taken for granted, the average man applauds the development of increasingly destructive weapons systems. He may recognize that the use of these weapons would probably mean the destruction of himself, his society, and perhaps the human race. But his thought starts from the premise that military force is essential to survival, and he cannot conceive of other alternatives. It is literally unthinkable to him that disarmament may be the only solution, so he can only laud every development in weaponry and hope that somehow the weapons will never be used.* [4]

And the weapons production continues, on the self-fulfilling belief that they act as a deterrent. When asked for proof, advocates point out, smugly, that a nuclear war hasn't happened yet. Nagasaki and Hiroshima aside, the mentality of successful deterrence is reminiscent of the people who used to toss salt all about the grounds of their homes each day to keep the tigers away. When informed that there were no tigers in the area, they responded, "Of course there aren't—the salt works doesn't it?"

As another example of the cultural assumption/ illusion effect, consider the following, provided by John Lilly:

> The God of Money has many demi-Gods below Him. One of these demi-Gods is banking. When one thinks about it, a bank is a very peculiar place. When one examines the operations that go on in a bank, as if he were a visitor from another planet, he sees a lot of people entering a building, going up to counters, writing out slips of paper, receiving other slips of paper, and sometimes the green paper that represents "money" itself (or the silver, or the gold). Some people, when you ask them what they are doing at a bank, will say, "I'm cashing a check," or "I'm depositing money I've earned," or "I'm establishing my credit." These are some of the rituals and litanies of the church of God as Money. A bank, then, represents a neighborhood church of this particular God, or perhaps one of the cathedrals of the Wall Street area.[5]

In our world—or our illusion, as you may care to see it—we have many idols, "simulations of God" as described by Lilly. These days we have many gods: a salary in the six figures, my country 'tis of thee, pills for pains, software and hardware, a body like the proverbial brick outhouse, scoring, the new celibacy, and a meaningful relationship. Even "a meaningful relationship with God"—that's a god in itself, particularly if it's a ritual or an obsession without thought. Spirituality it's not.

Spirituality is our ticket out of this world of illusion. A bit of detachment is necessary—you must be in this world but not of it. With spirituality, you can enrich yourself without having to give up your health club membership, your season tickets to the symphony, or your bowling league. But, on a daily basis, you must step back and realize that material attachments are only temporary, that death lurks around the corner.

When craving grows stronger, self-control is lost. When self-control is lost, craving grows stronger than ever. A man who lives thus will never escape the wheel of birth and death.

—SHANKARA

Yes, having a house with a pool is nice, and getting involved in office politics is interesting. But these things shouldn't be the end-all, be-all in your life. There are better riches to be had within yourself and, hence, to give to others.

But where shall wisdom be found? And where is the place of understanding? It cannot be gotten for gold, neither shall silver be weighed for the price thereof.

—THE BIBLE (JOB XXVIII, 12, 15)

Thus, detachment is the key. It is the mental process of drawing back, and it's not easy to achieve. You develop detachment by synthesizing the right information and realizations, and then by observing and monitoring yourself on a daily basis. Detachment entails non-identification. Responding rather than reacting. Reactions are automatic, responses take awareness.

Learn what is transient in life and what is enduring. Cars, jobs, houses, and jewels are only objects. Friendship, caring, love, respect, giving, and learning are the things people should spend more of their time, energy, and attention on. The only things that endure are the things that nourish the soul—nothing else.

60

More flesh, more worms;
More wealth, more worry;
More women, more witchcraft;
More concubines, more lechery;
More slaves, more thievery.
(But) More law, more life;
More study, more wisdom;
More counsel, more enlightenment;
More righteousness, more peace.

—THE TALMUD
(FROM MISHNA)

Use your brain in new ways. Try to break old thinking habits that inhibit or stop you from growing. Use your intuition more, rely less on your intellect and emotions. Their applications are worthy, but limited. Intuition can break illusion and let you perceive things as they truly are.

Learn the distinction between your two selves. The *object* part of you is oriented toward external things. It wants to *have*. It is often automatic and unaware. The *observing* part of you is the state of awareness. It is capable of disassociating itself from the object-self and can then observe it. The observing self takes in; it receives and is vigilant. It makes the connection with being. The object and observing selves have their parallel in the conventional and real selves:

It will suffice here to say that the perception of the reality of real self in contrast to conventional self may make us realize that what we ordinarily call real is just a fiction, what we call truth is false. What we call personality is really that which shadows our potential personality and is in fact that which deprives our inner growth. That which we call self is really that which veils our "self," and what to us is "we" is only a barrier to becoming "We." In short, from conventional "I" to real "I," from conventional "we" to real "We" is a long way to go which requires freeing ourselves of undesirable desires and undesirable attitudes.[6]

61

Stop and take a look at yourself. Are you real? Or do you go on perpetuating your own and the world's illusions?

NOTES

1   Deikman, Arthur, *The Observing Self*. Boston: Beacon Press, 1982, p. 119.
2   *Ibid,* p. 129.
3   Tart, Charles T., *States of Consciousness*. New York: Dutton, 1975 (original publisher), pp. 33–34. Now published by Psychological Processes, Box 3914, San Rafael, CA 94901.
4   Putney, Snell and Putney, Gail, *The Adjusted American*. New York: Harper and Row, 1964, pp. 6–7.
5   Lilly, John, *Simulations of God*. New York: Bantam, 1975, pp. 105–106.
6   Arasteh, A. Reza, *Growth in Selfhood*. London: Routledge and Kegan Paul, 1980, pp. 6–7.

chapter eight

brotherhood/sisterhood

*But whoso hath this world's good, and seeth his
brother have need, and shutteth up his bowels
of compassion from him, how dwelleth the love
of God in him?*

*My little children, let us not love in word
neither in tongue; but in deed and in truth.*
—I JOHN 3:17,18

What is thine is mine, and all mine is thine.
—PLAUTUS

Brotherly love is a virtue that's faced some pretty tough
times of late. On the one hand, it's described to us in infancy, in golden, honeyed tones. We are taught to reach for
it like some shiny bauble. On the other hand, the minute we
become a bit more mature, competitiveness and acquisition
are suddenly sprung on us as the new shiny baubles.

And what of brotherly love? Ask a man who's just
driven off the lot with his first brand new Mercedes if he's
pondering brotherly love as he tests the car's sun roof.
Chances are slim he's feeling sympathy for the poor man
who has to walk to work. Brotherly love? Check with the

developer who's planning to raze several blocks of low-income housing to build a high-rise office complex. Is he spending sleepless nights worrying about where the displaced and impoverished tenants are going to live? Or perhaps you'd like to discuss brotherly love with a terrorist who's setting off a bomb to call attention to some oblique political demands.

Brotherly love, it seems, has been relegated to a back seat in our Western society, overshadowed by more "important" virtues, such as success and achievement. It is something that most people seem to think should be left to the clergy and the bleeding heart liberals. But in these semi-troubled times, it is a virtue that more of us should attempt to practice.

Just what is brotherly love? Psychologist Erich Fromm, in his book *The Art of Loving,* distinguishes five varieties of love: love of God, self-love, erotic love, motherly love, and, of course, brotherly love. After love of God, Fromm has described brotherly love as being the most fundamental kind of love. One that transcends the individual and extends to all mankind. Brotherly love is caring, respecting, and wishing well to *everyone,* and not just the members of your aerobics class. According to Dr. Fromm, brotherly love is the "experience of union with all men, of human solidarity, of human atonement."

There it is—the key at-onement. Knowing in your heart (and not just with your keen intellectual faculties) that we are all *one,* that we are all equal in God's eyes (or, if you will, from some *higher perspective*). Brotherly love derives from humility; it sheds preoccupation with "me-ism." You can't just walk into a brotherly love boutique and buy it—you must experience it. And to experience it, you must first be able to understand it deeply, and second, you must perceive it around you.

Whenever the rabbi of Sasor saw anyone's suffering, either of spirit or of body, he shared it so earnestly that the other's suffering became his own. Once someone expressed his astonishment at this capacity to share in another's troubles. "What do you mean 'share'?" said the rabbi. "It is my own sorrow; how can I help but suffer it?"[1]

Okay, so how do you *understand* brotherly love? Perhaps spend a few hours volunteering for your local Salvation Army serving free lunches? It's a bit deeper than that. You must first comprehend the concept of the "Oversoul" or "Universal Soul" that is implied in all the major religions. We are all said to have a soul which is originated from the Oversoul. Our psychic connection—our equality to one another—derives from this concept (even though equality has been diluted in the last few centuries to mean equality as rights via the legal system).

The Oversoul is Truth or God. And as emphasized in the neo-Platonism of Alexandria, we have all dwelled in the Universal Soul or Truth. We all, at one time or another, have seen the face of Truth. What we today (and as always on earth) regard as truth, is merely a shadow of that which *shines above* in all its perfection. To regain this lost felicity is the true goal of spirituality and is ultimately the underlying goal of all religions. We are all in exile, then, from the Divine and from the perfection of brotherly love, and it is our mission to attempt a reunion.

We distinguish the announcements of the soul, its manifestations of its own nature, by the term Revelation. *These are always attended by the emotion of the sublime. For this communication is an influx of the Divine mind into our mind. . . . Everywhere, the history of religion betrays a tendency to enthusiasm. The rapture of the Moravian and Quietist; the opening of the internal sense of the Word, in the language of the New Jerusalem Church; the revival of the Calvinistic churches; the experiences of the Methodists, are varying forms of that shudder of awe and delight with which the individual soul always mingles with the universal soul.*[2]

Those are the words of Ralph Waldo Emerson, who, in

alluding to the meaning of brotherhood, continues, ". . . the heart in thee is the heart of all; not a valve, not a wall, not an intersection is there anywhere in nature, but one blood rolls uninterruptedly as an endless circulation through all men, as the water of the globe is all one sea, and truly seen, its tide is one."[3]

Those who can recognize the reality in Emerson's universal truisms are indeed lucky. Perhaps most of us—as we worry about our bills or figure out how much ground beef it takes to make meatloaf for six—have trouble connecting ourselves spiritually to a peanut vendor in Calcutta or neo-realist painter on the Left Bank. But the bottom line is that we are all one, despite our differences in race, nationality, features, IQ, income, and personality. As Fromm notes, "In order to experience this identity, it is necessary to penetrate from the periphery to the core. If I perceive in another person mainly the surface, I perceive mainly the differences, that which separates us. If I penetrate the core, I perceive our identity, the fact of our brotherhood."[4]

Brotherhood/sisterhood is a highly developed type of love—an extremely powerful bond that no creatures except our humble selves are capable of. Even animals, after all, "love" their offspring. But brotherly love is spiritual, as it goes beyond the baser, animal levels of mankind. One is able to give, and not just take; one is able to empathize with other human beings. In practicing brotherly love, you act not out of self-interest, but out of other-interest. This higher love is our greatest resource, our greatest gift. Yet, somehow it is the virtue that we most frequently fail to utilize. We've been conditioned to believe that if we show some compassion or brotherly love, we're being "naive" or are under the impression that someone will surely take advantage of us. The state of brotherhood in today's world is weak at best.

Take a look at what's going on around us. It's certainly not a misty-eyed view of brotherly love that's compelling the United States and the Soviet Union to spend huge sums of money so that they can destroy each other many times over. Meanwhile, a willing U.S. worker has difficulty finding a job, and alcoholism is a national pastime in the USSR. Somehow, someone must have forgotten the people who inhabit both places.

Somewhere along the line, manifestos took over and made the Soviets forget that we too fret over our children growing up too fast. At some time, government and power and lust to make the world safe for democracy made *us* forget that Soviets also wonder what they're going to fix for dinner. Somehow, it became *us* against *them,* and our differences loomed up as inevitably as death and taxes; our similarities suddenly became nil.

In reality, we are quite similar. Our governments and societies have their own strong points and weaknesses. Sure, there's much to be said about free enterprise, but what about the kid who spends thousands of dollars to go to college and then can't find a job? The Soviets find that aspect of our system incomprehensible. They tout communism and the idea that everything exists for the common good. But what about their preoccupation (and black market) for consumer goods? In the end, the common man *is* the same, whether we crave burgers or borscht.

But let's move our thoughts from the very large and global to the very small and local. Do we treat our friends and neighbors as cheap raw material? Are we any better in our attitudes during our daily lives than we are on that huge, impersonal, global level? We rarely stop to observe ourselves and our actions.

One writer, Leo Buscaglia, has pondered this subject, where, after quoting Confucius ("Why does the world create cares for itself?"), he notes,

This very human question continues to resound disturbingly in the minds of all of us as we engage in the daily processes of living. What is most disillusioning is that we seem to have come no closer to an answer over these thousands of years. Rather we have persisted in

abusing and killing ourselves and each other. More and more we appear to be losing the joy in spontaneity and the wonder in spirituality. We seem to have become alienated from the fact that we are all part of everything and everyone, and we have retreated into egocentricity and provincialism. As a result, we, and the world in which we live, still are mainly unrealized potential. We are all much less than what we can be.[7]

Again, we are not living up to our promise of brotherly love—our attainment of the divine. The absence of this spiritual value seems to be responsible for many of our daily stresses and is probably responsible for the crowded therapists' couches, though not all of these M.D.'s and Ph.D.'s recognize the reasons that the patients are there. We find a disheartening lack of quality in our social interactions and relationships. There's an underlying feeling of transience, of shallowness and not caring in our daily lives. Mental illness, alcoholism, drug abuse, delinquency, and criminal behavior have become some individuals' means of coping. This feeling of being disconnected or rootlessness seems to be most magnified in our male/female relationships. We seem to continually have trouble *relating* to one another. Relationships that begin with bombs bursting in mid-air and flowery sonnets end with legal representatives arguing about who gets the house. And people are more fearful than ever to get back into a relationship. It's a vicious cycle.

The absence of brotherly love rears its vacuous head in other matters of daily life. Money, for example, seems to stay in a very few lucky hands, and health is something we don't usually think about when we have it. If we're fortunate to be healthy, we don't tend to spend our spare time helping those who aren't, let alone think about them.

Essentially, the matter of brotherly love is a part of the larger matter of love itself. And love is the key element in all religions and spiritual systems. But though we hear, read, and talk about love all too much, how many practice it? When we consider the other forms of love mentioned by

Fromm—self-love, motherly love, erotic (or romantic) love, and the love of God—how *do* we fare?

By *self-love,* Fromm is implying self-affirmation, self-respect, or self-acceptance: "The idea expressed in the Biblical *Love they neighbor as thyself!* implies that respect for one's own integrity and uniqueness, love for and understanding of one's own self, cannot be separated from respect and love and understanding for another individual."[8] Fromm also notes the opposite—that narcissistic or selfish people are not only incapable of loving others, but are incapable of loving themselves. The antidote is *unselfishness,* which may lead to real self-love.

Motherly love, or parental love, seems to come easiest to most people, but Fromm notes that whereas most mothers are capable of loving their infant or young child, this is only because of instinct. It is something found everywhere in the animal world. It is therefore no major achievement. What differentiates the truly loving mother from those that falter at the task of motherhood becomes much clearer when the child begins to grow. "The narcissistic, the domineering, the possessive woman can succeed in being a *loving* mother as long as the child is small. . . . Motherly love for the growing child, love which wants nothing for itself, is perhaps the most difficult. . . . A woman can be a truly loving mother only if she can *love*; if she is able to love her husband, other children, strangers, all human beings."[9] Mothers who aren't "lovers" in this more general sense are the very same mothers who find it difficult to let go when the youngster grows up; they are generally incapable of or too weak to bear separation. In this sense, these women have actually become dependent upon their children, a potentially pathological situation.

Fromm sees *erotic love* as the "craving for complete fusion" or the desire to unite with another person. He also notes that erotic love can be the "most deceptive form of love there is." He rightly sees "falling in love" as typically short-lived, with many couples incapable of sustaining the bond beyond that stage, simply because they are unskilled in the "art of loving." The art of loving is akin to brotherly love. In Fromm's view, mates with the greatest success potential are those who not only share erotic or romantic love, but who are also capable of attaining the more general and more important form of love—brotherly love.

The *love of God* is the highest form of love, but, as Fromm notes, this has different meanings for different people. These differences may spring from a person's upbringing, cultural background, religious beliefs, and/or level of maturity. Yet the love of God has a universal basis in man's generalized need for love that ultimately stems from his experience of separateness and the associated need to overcome the anxiety of separateness by the experience of union. So, in effect, the love of God is similar in nature to the love of man. It was Mohammed who said, "Do you think you love your Creator? Love your fellow-creature first." In other words, to love God is to love the products of his creation. And further, when one reaches the level of maturity where one can relate to others as brothers (or sisters), one is then in a better position to understand God and his ways and, hence, to love God.

Love—especially brotherly love—is something we should be aware of as our potential, as our destiny. It should be a virtue—a way of life—that all of us strive for. Hence, by trying to understand the concept of brotherhood and then by practicing it, we are taking steps in the direction of a more spiritual life.

NOTES

1   Buber, Martin, *Tales of the Hasidim—Later Masters.* New York: Shocken Books, 1948, p. 86.
2   Emerson, Ralph Waldo, *Emerson's Essays.* New York: Thomas Y. Crowell, 1926, pp. 198–200.
3   *Ibid,* pp. 208–209.

4   Fromm, Erich, *The Art of Loving.* New York: Harper and Row, 1956, p. 41.

5   Buscaglia, Leo, *Personhood.* New York: Fawcett, 1978, p. ix.

6   Fromm, *op. cit.,* p. 49.

7   *Ibid,* pp. 43–44.

chapter nine

words and practice

If one of the brothers or one of the sisters is in
need of clothes and has not enough food to live on,
and one of you says to them, "I wish you well; keep
yourself warm and eat plenty," without giving them
these bare necessities of life, then what good is
that? Faith is like that: if good works do not
go with it, it is quite dead. . . . You see now
that it is by doing something good, and not only
by believing, that a man is justified. . . . A
body dies when it is separated from the spirit,
and in the same way faith is dead if it is separated
from good deeds.
—JAMES (2.15, 16, 24, 26)

We tell ourselves daily lies to get by. That's just the way we live, it seems. When we stare at ourselves naked in the mirror, we overlook that extra five pounds clinging tenaciously to our waistlines. On the job, we turn in a less-than-spectacular project and tell ourselves that it's okay, that no one expects anything more. In romance, when we don't give 100 percent to the other person, we pretend that we're tired or too busy. We proclaim we are liberals and unprejudiced, but privately rant about neighborhoods "going black" or about Jews "controlling business."

Somehow, on the path from innocence and infancy to adulthood, we have lost much of our basic honesty, both with ourselves and with others. And this loss of honesty, this daily deception, is destructive and unhealthy.

Lack of honesty is not just negative on an everyday basis: it stunts our spiritual growth. All great religions and spiritual systems claim that the first step toward spirituality is sincerity—both with yourself ("knowing thyself") and others. Taken further, this sincerity should extend beyond words into action. It can be as simple as telling someone you'll be at his house at a certain time and then *being* there, or it can be as complex as a politician promising less unemployment and then making good on his promise. This honesty makes for a better, more trusting, and, yes, more spiritual world.

Let us quickly point out that we are not advocates of total and brutal honesty. This can be just as destructive as lying. The Little White Lie has done much to further civilization, we admit. What good does it do to tell someone to his or her face that their personalities are about as interesting as stale bread? Not much.

However, deception and lying are so widespread in our culture that we usually take it for granted; we are immune to it. We hear an advertising pitch on television for the "best" detergent, but we don't run to the FCC charging that the advertising is false. Our mate tells us that he/she loves only us, but we don't make them cross the Sahara barefoot to prove their love. As children, when we heard about Santa Claus, few of us went to great lengths to dispute it.

But eventually, this chronic fibbing catches up on us and causes us discord in varying degrees. Both in our personal lives and on the job, we feel this discord often when we say one thing ("Sure, I'd love to go to Podunk on a business trip . . .") and really mean something else ("I have seniority! Why can't the new kid go?"). The discord is also felt when we say one thing and do another ("People pay too much attention to status goods" you say, while adjusting your Piaget watch). This discord, this fear of being ourself, causes many problems, including a lack of self-trust and stress. At its extremes, it can produce mental illness. Unless you are sound psychologically, it is difficult to pursue spiritual goals. In order to grow a garden of flowers, one must pull weeds and prepare the soil first. Thus, with spirituality, one must first have the mental capacity and self-understanding before these goals can be attained.

Schizophrenia is a severe, albeit common, form of mental illness distinguished by withdrawal, delusions, bizarre mannerisms, and thought disturbance. Psychologists have depicted schizophrenia as a severe ego weakness coupled with difficulty in social communication. A popular theory of schizophrenia (especially childhood schizophrenia) is known as the double-bind theory. Schizophrenics tend to communicate in a form of double talk, and three investigators, Gregory Bateson, Don Jackson, and Jay Haley, have posited their double-bind theory: the schizophrenic's double talk (and its related symptoms) is caused by double talk.

Double-talk communication is learned early in family life. Typically, the "cause" is a parent, often the mother ("schizophrenogenic mother" is a common psychiatric term). These parents of schizophrenics generally exhibit severe insecurities themselves; they are almost totally estranged from their "real" selves and their "real" feelings. Therefore, the parents pass these double messages on to their children. It's the old "damned if you do, damned if you don't" message that the children pick up. The parent may profess love toward the child overtly but is inwardly rejecting the child. The child may be shoved aside as he tries to return and respond to this "love." Over a period of years, this deception repeats itself, and the youngster becomes understandably confused as to what is or is not reality. The child senses the discrepancy between the overt communication and metacommunication and, after a while, doesn't know whether he's coming or going.

This double-bind theory emphasizes the fact that the discrepancy between inner and outer selves in social interactions can be not only stressful, but that it can also lead to emotional disturbance in certain individuals. We're not saying that just because you profess to "love" your job and are actually bored with it, you will find yourself naked and screaming on a window ledge high above the city. But lies to yourself do produce mental and emotional stress.

All of which brings us to the subject of roles and role-playing—our public selves. People often become the roles they play because they are so good at performing in this theater of life. Research by psychologist Mark Snyder, as reported in a March 1980 *Psychology Today* article, further illustrates this. The article, "The Many Me's of The Self Monitor," describes individuals who are "keenly aware of the impression they are making and constantly fine-tuning their performance." While most of us are self-monitors to some degree ("Does my clothing look professional?" "Am I acting too silly at this office party?") Snyder notes that high self-monitors are those whose "true self" is virtually indistinguishable from the social roles they play. If you are wondering whether you are a high or low self-monitoring individual (or somewhere in between), you might wish to take the simple test devised by Snyder and provided below.

These statements concern personal reactions to a number of different situations. No two statements are exactly alike, so consider each statement carefully before answering. If a statement is true, or mostly true, as applied to you, circle the T. If a statement is false, or not usually true, as applied to you, circle the F.

1. *I find it hard to imitate the behavior of other people.*   *T F*

2. I guess I put on a show to impress or
   entertain people.   T   F

3. I would probably make a good actor.   T   F

4. I sometimes appear to others to be
   experiencing deeper emotions than I
   actually am.   T   F

5. In a group of people I am rarely the center
   of attention.   T   F

6. In different situations and with different
   people, I often act like very different
   persons.   T   F

7. I can only argue for ideas I already believe.   T   F

8. In order to get along and be liked, I tend to
   be what people expect me to be rather than
   anything else.   T   F

9. I may deceive people by being friendly when
   I really dislike them.   T   F

10. I'm not always the person I appear to be.   T   F

SCORING: Give yourself one point for each of questions 1, 5 and 7 that you answered F. Give yourself one point for each of the remaining questions that you answered T. Add up your points. If you are a good judge of yourself and scored 7 or above, you are probably a high self-monitoring individual; 3 or below, you are probably a low self-monitoring individual.

According to Snyder, low self-monitors are less conforming and are less affected by differences in social settings, and "their self-presentations were more accurate reflections of their personal attitudes and dispositions." In other words, a low self-monitor is more likely to tell his or her employer that a business trip to Podunk is boring and worthless.

Interestingly, high self-monitors (he or she would take

the boring trip to Podunk because it "looked good") tend to prefer low self-monitors as friends—possibly because high self-monitors are more comfortable being around persons less interested in impression management. Nonetheless, Snyder also notes that high self-monitors are not as adept at disclosing private feelings or opinions, and that this could be emotionally unhealthy.

"Yet, it is almost a canon of modern psychology that a person's ability to reveal a *true self* to intimates is essential to emotional health," Snyder writes. High self-monitors can be easily understood within the view of human nature espoused by sociologist Erving Goffman. For Goffman, "the world of appearances appears to be all" (a theory that is in agreement with Shakespeare's "All the world is a stage."). Goffman sees social interactions as "a theatrical performance in which each individual acts out a 'line.' " According to Goffman, we are the sum of our various performances. Thus, if we play enough young executive roles, we will eventually become young executives. If we play the rejected job applicant often enough, we will become just that.

Claude M. Steiner, an associate of the late Eric Berne (father of Transactional Analysis) has taken Goffman's philosophy one step further and has made it into an art form. In Steiner's Book, *Scripts People Live,* games and life scripts are said to be the two key facets in people's behavior. Games (besides Monopoly) are particular interpersonal transactions with a particular theme. For example, there's the "pity me" game an employee may play with an employer, in which the employer feels guilty and/or sympathetic toward the employee and forks out more money or gives the employee less work.

A life script may comprise a series of related games but is better described by Steiner as a "complex set of transactions, by nature recurrent, but not necessarily recurring since a complete performance may require a whole lifetime." Steiner believes that everyone has a life script, something that derives from decisions made in childhood and that is fortified by pressure from parents and other adults. Your life script may be to run your own small business, it may be to become a powerful politician, or it may be to become a celebrity or to get married to a nice person and have an endless stream of nice kids.

At some point, however, the script takes over and becomes your personality. You *become* that powerful politician or that Wall Street prodigy. Typically you lose sight of your true self, and there's a lingering sense of emptiness. It's not unusual to build yourself a mental and behavioral prison with your scripts. Steiner and other TA therapists use a method known as script analysis that allows one to gain greater insight into the subtleties of one's life script and, therefore, to learn how to break out of the play.

In any case, the bottom line is honesty. If you can be that Wall Street whiz kid and still be true to yourself and to others, all the better. But for most of us, those little lies we weave cause us some degree of anguish. By gaining insight into our life's scripts, perhaps we can free ourselves from them. We can then become more open, honest, and spontaneous. Our interactions with other people will also benefit.

chapter ten

to be human again

*To love God truly, one must
first love man. And if anyone
tells you that he loves God and
does not love his fellow-man, you
will know that he is lying.*

—MARTIN BUBER

Just about everyone is raised with some form of religion influencing them. It may be orthodox Catholicism, with rosaries and confessions, or perhaps just a light touch of Presbyterianism, attending a service now and then, at Easter or Christmas. In any case, we learn the rules and hymns, the beliefs, and when to kneel. No matter how you look at it, we get somewhat programmed. Few of us escape those influences.

Those who do make a conscious effort to escape, often do a complete turn around. Once they become disenchanted with religious rules, ritual, and morality, they'll frequently become agnostic or—a step further—atheistic. Others may explore non-Western religions or, if they desire something totally different, join a local cult. At least then they *really* wouldn't have to think.

Recently, more people, turned off by orthodox traditions and so-called "irrelevant" morality taught by mainline churches, have become interested in humanism, a philosophy that in many ways could be more *spiritual* than some forms of organized religion. A humanist could be a religious person or not. It doesn't matter. Humanists emphasize the positive aspects of man rather than keeping the negative aspects in check with fire and brimstone. They believe in mankind's potential and maintain that organized religion is essentially a political institution, functioning to diminish man's true nature. Humanism is essentially an affirmation of life and human values. In this sense, humanists are actually closer to the original intent and spirit of all world religions than are today's organized, corporate religions.

Humanism actually had its beginnings in the late Middle Ages and continued into the Age of Enlightenment. In his book, *To Have Or To Be?*, psychologist Erich Fromm notes that the dehumanization of the social character and the parallel rise of the industrial and cybernetic revolutions led to a protest movement and the emergence of a new humanism. The protest found expression among theistic Christians as well as pantheists and nontheistic philosophies. Humanism continued in various forms past the Age of Enlightenment and is presently experiencing a major revival within the format of psychology.

Humanistic psychology received its initial impetus in the ideas and works of Erich Fromm, when, as far back as 1947 (*Man For Himself: An Inquiry Into the Psychology of Ethics*), Fromm advocated "humanistic ethics," an applied science—the art of living and loving. The art of living and loving required a theoretical science of human functioning, and this science was psychology. The key to the success of present and future humanity, according to Fromm, lies deep within the human psyche in man's unlimited, higher potentials.

Following (and continuing with) Fromm, humanistic

psychology (or modern humanism) received its greatest impetus in the works of two American psychologists, Carl R. Rogers and Abraham Maslow. Rogers emphasized that we all have a real self that lies dormant behind our conditioned, secondary self, and, that with proper self-work, the real or potential self can emerge. Maslow made the first major effort to move away from negative or illness-oriented conceptions of human personality, while emphasizing the positive. He is best known for his studies of "self-actualizing people" (e.g., Schweitzer, Einstein, etc.) and his "hierarchy of needs." Maslow envisions man as being able to grow through five levels of ascending sets of needs: physiological, safety, social, self-esteem, and self-actualization. While most people (and most societies as well) rarely achieve the fifth level of self-actualization, the potential is latent within everyone.

Maslow's hierarchy of needs is paralleled by a later formulation in the works of psychologist Lawrence Kohlberg. As the result of his extensive studies, Kohlberg arrived at a theory of moral development that delineates six ascending stages: *obedience* (resulting from threat of punishment); *egotistic orientation* (cooperative behavior for purposes of self-interest); *conformity* to social standards; *integration* into social institutions; an understanding of social contracts and the meaning of *commitments;* and *conscience* development as a universal principle. While the first four stages are attained by most culturally conditioned citizens, the last two stages are arrived at through personal effort and a higher awareness of the essential, universal principles of human existence.

Humanistic psychology sees itself as "third force" psychology, not wishing to align itself with dry behaviorism or illness-oriented psychologies (such as psychoanalysis). Modern humanistic psychology is primarily dedicated to the advancement of higher human capabilities: creativity, autonomy, courage, play, authenticity, warmth, love, and transcendent experiences.

Despite the positive image humanism seems to set forth, it is not without its detractors, namely those who go by the literal interpretation of the Bible, rather than by a psycho-spiritual interpretation. The anti-humanistic Moral Majority, which frequently hit the headlines a few years ago, is an indication of this detraction on a large scale. Their official president, Jerry Falwell, recently endorsed a best-selling book entitled *The Battle For the Mind*, by Pastor Tim LaHaye. In it, LaHaye writes, "Most people today do not realize what humanism really is and how it is destroying our culture, families, country—and one day, the entire world. Most of the evils in the world today can be traced to humanism, which has taken over our government, the UN, education, TV, and most of the influential things of life."[1]

Pastor LaHaye is the founder of the San Diego Christian Unified School System and Christian Heritage College. One wonders how LaHaye would react to the following, taken from *Love and Living*, written by one of the most important Christian writers of our age, Thomas Merton: "No humanism has retained the respect for man in his personal and existential actuality to the same extent as Christian humanism."[2]

LaHaye also states, "Humanism is a man-centered, philosophy that attempts to solve the problems of man and the world independently of God."[3] In discussing humanism, Merton notes, however, that its central idea is that ". . . God is love, not infinite power. Being Love, God has given himself without reservation to man so that he has become man. . . . The love which is also the infinite creative secret of God in his hidden mystery becomes manifest and active, through man, in man's world."[4]

Finally, the Moral Majority prides itself in its patriotism, and doesn't try to hide it: "At the risk of being accused of nationalistic pride, I would point out that had it not been for the Christian influence in America, our contemporary world would have completely lost the battle for the mind and would doubtless live in a totalitarian, one-world, humanistic state."[5] In discussing the "humanism of the Second Vatican Council" and its "Constitution on the Church in the Modern World," Merton (*Love and Living*), notes that, "The Christian is reminded that his allegiance is first of all to the entire human family, and that he must not appeal to Christian principles in order to justify a patriotism which, in fact, is dangerous or harmful to the universal good of the human race."[6]

Humanism, however, continues to flourish. A more recent outgrowth of humanistic psychology is that of *transpersonal psychology:* the science and study of spiritual experience and spiritual systems or paths. The emphasis is upon cross-cultural studies and upon the idea of universal man. Of very special interest to transpersonal psychologists are the ancient, esoteric systems of Eastern psychospirituality, namely Yoga, Hinduism, Taoism, Confucianism, Zen, Buddhism, Sufism, and Christian and Jewish mysticism. Congruent with their studies of Eastern systems, transpersonal psychologists are concerned with altered or higher states of consciousness, the essential issues or questions of existence, and the purpose and meaning of life and the universe. The key reference is *Transpersonal Psychologies,* edited by psychologist Charles Tart. The book contains excellent articles on each of the various Eastern systems of thought and practice by eminent authorities and also includes three valuable essays by Tart himself.

While, as suggested, all of the articles in Tart's book are of value, one entitled "Psychology and the Christian Mystical Tradition," by William McNamara, is especially noteworthy, in light of our present discussion. First, part of Father McNamara's biographical description:

> As a result of his extensive experience as spiritual director for hundreds of people, Father William discovered that American needed a brand new kind of contemplative life, less structured and regimented than the traditional Trappists ,Carmelites, or Camoldolese: a contemplative life that would be open to men and women

alike, young and old, clergy and lay, Christian and non-Christian, each participant fitting not into preestablished molds worked out over centuries but living out his contemplative calling in a more personal, existential, and contemporary eremetical manner.[7]

Next, let us represent, verbatim, the following, provided by Father William under the heading: "Current Activity: The Failure of Christianity":

We should be able to contact the living tradition of Christian Mysticism wherever there are Christians. This is not the case, however, because of the failure of Christianity.

If men who profess the faith are not drawn and captivated by the infinitely attractive Christ, then Christianity has failed.

If even morally upright men do not enjoy God, then Christianity has failed.

If even cold-bloodedly dutiful men have lost their taste and capacity for God, then Christianity has failed.

If God is not real enough to absorb in contemplation even the ecclesiastical leaders of the Church, then Christianity has failed.

If schools, parishes, convents, seminaries, and monasteries throughout our land are not at least half full of mystics—that is, people who know God by experience—then Christianity has failed.

If Christians are not, as a rule, more human, more integrated personalities because of their Christian spirit, then Christianity has failed.

The implication in each one of these instances, is, of course, that Christianity has indeed failed. It has not failed finally, in the sense that it is all over, and the battle is lost: but it is failing in its mission here and now.

The mission of Christianity is to enable man to see God and to be with God. Christ is the supreme and most complete revelation of religious truth, of love, of the Godhead. He who sees Christ, sees God; who enjoys Him enjoys God; who does His will does the will of his Father.

It is the mission of Christianity to keep the image of Christ alive and bright enough for men to see, to contemplate; and to keep the presence of Christ concrete, strong, and compelling enough for man to desire and achieve vital union.

It is here, precisely, where Christianity has failed. It has, over the centuries, become so completely absorbed in jobs to be done— admittedly vastly important jobs—that it has neglected its mission. [8]

The key point to understand here is that the spiritual quest begins *within,* essentially as the search for meaning, truth, and knowledge (something you cannot buy). Spirituality is least likely to be found lurking underneath a pew at your church or synagogue. You must transform the inner person. No amount of hymn-singing or prayer alone will achieve that. Whether you attain it through organized religion or philosophical humanism (or through some other means) is up to you. To become more spiritual, become more human.

NOTES

1   LaHaye, Tim, *The Battle For The Mind.* Old Tappan, N.J.: Revell, 1980, p. 9.
2   Merton, Thomas, *Love and Living.* New York: Bantam, 1979, p. 134.
3   LaHaye, *op. cit.,* p. 27.
4   Merton, *op. cit.,* p. 134.
5   LaHaye, *op. cit.,* p. 35.
6   Merton, *op. cit.,* p. 146.
7   McNamara, William, "Psychology and the Christ in Mystical Religion." In Tart, Charles T. (editor), *Transpersonal Psychologies.* El Cerrito, CA: Psychological Processes, 1983.
8   *Ibid,* pp. 429–430.

chapter eleven

creative consciousness

Be ye lamps unto yourselves.
Be your own reliance.
Hold to the truth within yourselves
As to the only lamp.
—BUDDHA

There's this car that you want—a sporty little convertible. You don't exactly have the money for it, but within a week you've managed to finance it and are feeling the wind twirling your tresses. You move into a new house with a backyard that looks like a garbage dump. A year later, it's a mini Garden of Eden, with vibrant plants coaxed out of the ground by your own loving persistence. You are a writer, working on a book. A blank page faces you for three weeks. But eventually, the book is finished.

In all of the aforementioned cases, the creative mind is busily (and often unconsciously) at work. Creativity is a fundamental life force, one that has advanced humanity from prehistoric cave dwellers to svelte, fashionable professionals who have standing appointments at their hair salons. Yet, not only is creativity often taken for granted, but we also overlook the fact that there are virtually no limits to how creative our minds can be.

It may take some by surprise, but one does not have to be a genius or particularly dynamic to be creative. Creativity often works in strange, unspoken ways.

A few years ago, John B. Calhoun, a research psychologist, spent a great deal of time studying the effects of crowding on the behavior of mice. At the National Institute of Mental Health's animal farm in Maryland, Calhoun devised living quarters for the rodents that were not much different from the overcrowded, cramped conditions that can be found for humans in large cities such as Tokyo or New York. After awhile, Calhoun's mice exhibited unusual behaviors such as homosexuality, overaggressiveness, eating disturbances, and maternal abnormalities.

While observing this veritable rat-race, Calhoun was able to identify two socially distinct types of mice: the high socializers and the low socializers. The high socializers were able to procure the best nesting sites, were effective in guarding them, were the first at the feeders, and had the greatest number of offspring. The low socializers were last at the feeders and water, had poor nesting sites, and were poor parents. In general, they were very unaggressive.

In line with Darwinian theory of natural selection, Calhoun predicted that low-social velocity mice would eventually be genetically eliminated because they were less effective and produced less offspring in comparison to the high-social velocity mice. Much to his surprise, there was the same ratio of high- to low-social velocity mice in generation after generation observed.

This being an interesting contradiction to Darwinian theory, Calhoun sought an explanation. He observed the low-social velocity mice more closely, and noticed that they had devised some rather unconventional (for rodents, that is) behaviors that allowed them to subsist.

For example, since all the choice addresses for nesting

sites were already taken, the low socializers were forced to burrow into the ground (made of a special granular material). However, if they burrowed in their usual manner, the hole would merely collapse on itself. Eventually, these mice devised something novel. They urinated on a particular spot, gathered the material up into a wet clump, and moved it aside, leaving a nice nesting hole.

Dr. Hugh Drummond, in an article entitled "Evolution: Survival of the Schleps" (*Mother Jones,* December, 1980), concluded that Calhoun's low-social velocity mice (he called them "schleps" and "schlimazels") survived despite the odds because they were *creative*.

"Think about it," he says in the article. "Why should the winners find new ways of coping with the environment when they do just fine with the old ways? The schlimazels have no choice; they have to be creative."

In our daily life, when we too schlep around like burrowing rodents, we are being much more creative than we realize. When we encounter a problem, everything from a car's gas gauge that says "E" to a major trauma, such as the death of a loved one, we find ways of coping. We are creative. But we should be putting our creativity to use much more often. It is possible.

In considering the relationships between spirituality, religion, and creativity or discovery, the links are manifold. First, it is important to realize that organized or institutionalized religion has, in the past, and for good reason, gained the reputation of being counter-creative and anti-discovery. Throughout history, many great discoveries and creative, scientific theories have met strong, religious resistance. A classic example from history is the vehement objection by the Church to Copernicus (and later, Galileo) and his heliocentric theory of the movement of planets around the sun. Not only was the clergy so narrow-minded that they could not see fit to acknowledge the theory, but they were also so egocentric and arrogant that they refused to even look through the telescope! And the same resistance continues to the present day, with the creation/evolution controversy a blatant example.

On the other hand, it is noteworthy that practically every famous scientist who has ever made a significant discovery or formulated a major new theory admitted to being religious. A close look at their personal accounts or biographies reveals they tended to believe in a personal God and, in this sense, are better described as being spiritual. Even Darwin, who was opposed by the formal Church and was accused of being atheistic, was a spiritual person, as witnessed in his *Origin of Species* where in the very last sentence of the book he writes, "There is grandeur in this [evolutionary] view of life, with its several powers, having been originally breathed by the Creator into a few forms or into one; and that, whilst this planet has gone cycling on according to the fixed law of gravity, from so simple a beginning endless forms most beautiful and most wonderful have been, and are being evolved."[1] Darwin, like all true spiritualists merely chose to take the Bible figuratively (psychologically or symbolically) rather than literally or concretely.

Actually, creativity is an inherent aspect of spirituality. Possibly the most fundamental statement made in the Bible is that man is made in the image of God: "Then God said, 'Let us make man in our image, after our likeness; and let them have dominion over the fish of the sea, and over the birds of the air, and over the cattle, and over all the earth, and over every creepling that creeps upon the earth.' So God created man in his own image, in the image of God he created him; male and female he created them (Gen. 1:26-27)."

The intimate relation between creativity and spirituality, within the context of "man is made in the image and likeness of God," is nicely elaborated upon by Matthew Fox in his book, *Compassion*:

This tradition that all are creators is a profoundly Biblical tradition as well. When Genesis declares that God made humanity in "the image and likeness of God," it declares that all are artists. After all, the entire story in Genesis that precedes the imago dei *is all about one aspect of God: God as Creator. The Spirit hovering over the waters that initiates the birth of all that exists from light to humankind. To be an "image and likeness" of the Creator is to be a creator.*[2]

Fox then goes on to amplify upon another theme we support: all of us are creative, and creativity is not something existing in a vacuum or merely in the artist's studio.

Some people are creators as parents, some as mechanics or repairers of industrial parts, others are carpenters, lovers, cooks, gardeners, teachers, thinkers, dancers, musicians, story-tellers, laughers, counselors, or some combination of all these or of others. Creativity is not limited to an elitist field called "the Arts"; it is much more important than that. Art is not for art's sake but for ecstasy's sake. . . . Art is for people's sake. Creativity is everybody's and affects all of us. . . . If creativity is a spirituality then it is with us at some level and in some way all our day long. It becomes a way we feel and see the world and allow the world to feel and see us. It is essentially non-elitist."[3]

Fox also asks the pertinent question, "The notion that creativity might be everyone's possession and prerogative and not that of an elitist few has not been preached from the housetops of late. But is it an idea whose time has come? Are the compulsions of overwork and of competition . . . related to a common *flight from creativity*? If so, then underemployment and unemployment are also related to a flight from creativity."[4] He further notes that creativity is a double edged sword in that it can be utilized for good or evil: "One might say that our medieval ancestors who invented torture instruments for the Inquisition as well as our present Pentagon employees who invented napalm or herbicides to kill all vegetation were being 'creative.' "[5]

There are many books that have been written on the

subject of creativity, most of them of value. As mentioned earlier, creativity is inherent in human nature, and hence the creative process may be found everywhere, in all forms of activity. Its highest products are also found in the most diverse fields, including visual art (painting, film, drawing, sculpture, crafts), architecture, poetry, cooking, theater, music, dance, philosophy, science, and invention. Most books on the subject of creativity agree that, while we *all* are capable of being creative, most of us are inhibited by false assumptions and unfounded fears. Most false assumptions center around the idea that creativity is elitist and that one needs special talents before he or she can be creative. We have already dispelled the elitist assumption, and as to talent, most authorities agree that while in certain cases this may be a factor, we all have creative talent; however, its unfolding requires motivation or desire, information and orientation, concentration, training, learning, practice, self-confidence, and patience. And all of these qualities, if not already being actualized, can be developed. Associated fears include: fear of being different (due to conformity), fear of failure (or success), fear of criticism and rejection, and fear of trying something new, unfamiliar, or different. And, like practically all fears, these fears are imagined and have no base in reality. As Banks, Belleston, and Edwards, in their book entitled *Design Yourself!*, emphasize, "Creativity may just be a matter of getting rid of something."

Creativity is also an essential part of living. "Creative living" is a common expression these days, but it should be able to go beyond the expressive or "buzz word" stage. As an example of *art in living* (and its kinship to loving), everyone should read Erich Fromm's *The Art of Loving*. He explains quite clearly that "This attitude—that nothing is easier than to love—has continued to be the prevalent idea about love in spite of the overwhelming evidence to the contrary. . . . The first step is to become aware that *love is an art,* just as living is an art; if we want to learn how to love we must proceed in the same way we have to proceed if we want to learn any other art, say music, painting, carpentry, or the art of medicine or engineering."[6] And love, to be learned, must above all be practiced. The practice of love, Fromm points out, entails the same requirements as found in the practice of any other art: discipline, concentration, patience, supreme concern, and though not necessarily found in the practice of other arts, but probably significant in many respects, the overcoming of one's narcissism. One should strive to overcome pure subjectivity and to become objective. Humility and the appropriate use of reason should also be involved in this endeavor. Since the fine art and practice of love can accompany growth (spiritual growth), "the process of emergence, of birth, of waking up, requires one quality as a necessary condition: *faith*. The practice of the art of loving requires the practice of faith."[7] And, according to Fromm, the basis of rational faith is "productiveness." By productiveness, Fromm means that we harness our most positive and most beneficial human potentialities. Furthermore, the practice of love requires courage and a sense of fairness and justice.

Fromm emphasizes why people as a whole (especially people in the West) have not progressed very far in understanding and learning the fine art of loving:

> *Could it be that only those things are considered worthy of being learned with which one can earn money or prestige, and that love, which "only" profits the soul, but is profitless in the modern sense, is a luxury we have no right to spend much energy on?*[8]

Maybe so, but what a juxtaposition of values! As already touched upon elsewhere in this book, "We only possess that which will survive a shipwreck." And that includes those things that embellish our soul and nothing else— creative expression is undoubtedly one of these things.

One of the finest theories of evolution ever set forth is French philosopher Henri Bergson's notion of Creative

Evolution (in a book of the same title). Essentially, in disagreement with Darwinian theories of evolution that emphasize fortuitous selection and accidental mutation, Bergson proposes that evolution is purpose and goal oriented. It is not preplanned in the sense that it unfolds according to a set blueprint or design, but it entails a creative interplay (much like the development of a fine work of art) between the mind, conscious efforts of the organism, and external, higher, cosmic forces or influences. Bergson's theory is in line with ideas concerning higher human development and evolution found in ancient, esoteric, Eastern systems of thought and practice. And undoubtedly the highest human act of creative expression can be seen, in this perspective, as the desire and effort put forth in the quest for personal, spiritual development.

As one brilliant writer (A. Reza Arasteh, *Growth To Selfhood*) has pointed out,

> *My basic premise . . . is that the root of man's religious, philosophical, scientific, and artistic knowledge is creative experience. In fact, what differentiates man from beast is his creative vision. It is the formation of creative vision and objectivization of form which expands consciousness. . . . In fact it is the common denominator of all mankind. It is characterized by action for the sake of action, for the sake of the beloved, for the sake of someone, or some ideals outside of ourselves. It is self-explanatory, self-directing, self-forming, and self-expanding.* [9]

NOTES

1   Darwin, Charles, *The Origin of Species*. New York: New American Library, 1958, p. 450.
2   Fox, Matthew. *Compassion*. Minneapolis: Winston Press, 1979, p. 108.
3   *Ibid*, pp. 108–109.
4   *Ibid*, p. 106.
5   *Ibid*, p. 108.

6   Fromm, Erich, *The Art of Loving*. New York: Harper and Row, 1956, p. 4.

7   *Ibid.*

8   *Ibid,* p. 5.

9   Arasteh, A. Reza, *Growth to Selfhood*. London: Routledge and Kegan Paul, 1980, p. 107.

chapter twelve

service

*Why stand we here trembling around calling on
God for help, and not ourselves, in whom God
dwells, stretching a hand to save
the falling Man?*
—WILLIAM BLAKE

A woman in her mid-thirties sells radio time for a popular
FM station in a large city. She's excellent at her job, makes a
lot of money, and is respected by many. She also happens to
hate her work. It is a daily effort for her to get psyched up to
go out and sell. At home, she is bogged down with her
personal problems.

Another woman in that same market produces a radio
program for the blind. She goes to work each day with zest,
loving every detail of her employment. She can hardly work
enough.

Who has the most inner peace? The woman who loves
her work and whose work happens to benefit (even if in
only a small way) someone else. The key word here is
service—when preoccupation with one's self diminishes
and something greater, even perhaps spiritual, takes over.
It can occur on the job, at home, amongst friends, or within

the community. Service happens when someone sticks their neck out just a little bit more because they have a sense of mission, not just for money or attention.

Unfortunately, most of us tend to splash around in mediocrity for large portions of our lives. We live in our own little worlds, preoccupied with paying off our Mastercards, getting terminally depressed when our boss criticizes a project, and wondering how many weeks of dieting will produce a more svelte self. We tend to center all of our activities around our selves.

Yet we all have probably felt that intense rush of "goodness" when we have done something completely unselfish that benefits someone else or a group. Perhaps it was something as simple as giving up a bus seat for an elderly person or something as lofty as getting some legislation you really believed in passed. When this happens, we like to think that we have transcended our sometimes greedy, grubby selves into something higher—we have performed a service. While this is, of course, laudable, we can do even better. If we gain great satisfaction from helping others, we aren't serving them, we're simply serving ourselves. The key to service is understanding just what service is. Once we understand, we realize that service is simply a natural aspect of being human. It need not result in self-congratulation.

In his book, *The Sky's the Limit,* Dr. Wayne Dyer writes about an "ultimate sense of mission," the involvement in a personal cause that transcends or bypasses the self. This is the feeling that you, as one single person on this earth, in this universe, can *make a difference.* He believes (as do many others) that we all can discover a special purpose for ourselves, a way to be of service to others. In his own case, Dr. Dyer writes books for ordinary people—books that are interesting and entertaining yet contain a wealth of valuable ideas for improving one's self and one's life. By writing these books, Dr. Dyer believes he is fulfilling a purpose, and, more importantly, he notes that the adulation and approval he receives is quite secondary, for ". . . I would go right on writing and working without it," but only because of his knowledge "that I am an instrument of help to others."

Why not put a little more service—a sense of mission—into your life? Perhaps first you should gain some insight into your life's script (Chapter 8). Unless you happen to be a Dominician monk, most people's roles are purely in the service of survival and pleasure and the vigorous avoidance of pain. Yet this is a form of conditioning, of rigid programming, on how to lead your entire life. It is a mental and behavioral prison, not much better than the caste system found in ant and bee colonies, where the insect's official role becomes quite automatic and fixed: no freedom. With this rigid programming, you are merely using your *animal* brain and about ten percent of your *human* brain's capacity. Survival is the sole name of the game, and if you as well as others survive, chances are your culture will also survive.

Without service, however, our culture will not *thrive*. The step-up to service is an advance in human evolution. We all have the capacity to serve and with service comes fulfillment, which is more than mere satisfaction or even happiness.

Service is primarily an attitude, a state of mind, that can be achieved by anyone. You don't have to be Albert Schweitzer's descendant. You can achieve it without abandoning your family, your vocation, your house, or your hot tub. Martyrdom is not required. It is an attitude that can be put to use on a daily basis, and it can operate on any level. A person volunteering a few hours each day in a children's hospital is performing just as great a service as is Sister Teresa, the Nobel Prize winner, with her work in India. A hard-working volunteer for the March of Dimes might as well be Jonas Salk inventing the polio vaccine. Service entails compassion. It can operate within any sphere of life, large or small, acknowledged or not.

True service is not doing something only for reward or

approval. It's not when you volunteer to stay late to work on a company project so that you can get a good crack at a hefty raise. It's not joining a charity group so that you can see your name in the paper. With true service, you transcend yourself. You are engaged in an activity that implies that you are making a difference. You are doing something because you perceive that it is contributing to the collective welfare. At its best, it is carried out silently or anonymously and produces its own intrinsic fulfillment.

chapter thirteen

consciousness evolving

Serene will be our days and bright
And happy will our nature be,
When love is an unerring light,
And joy its own security.
—WILLIAM WORDSWORTH

Before you seek Aladdin's Lamp,
Ponder long on your wishes.
—SAYING

In a realm and a time both different from and like our own, there was an amazing electronic apparatus that was created in the hope of diverting the total collapse of society.

For no established reason (some theorists said "evil vibrations" were emanating from a nearby star system and others blamed climatic changes), the inhabitants of this world changed in a relatively short span of time from a peaceful and productive race of beings into an aggressive, covetous, and increasingly nihilistic race. The old representative form of government, which had maintained egalitarian law and custom, was brought down by a factionalized and largely chaotic revolution. At length, a powerful enclave of militia and intelligentsia gained control and announced the onset of marshal law and contingency plans to reestablish peace and prosperity.

The new regime rapidly consolidated its power, and the bulk of the populace outwardly encouraged the new government. Yet the leaders sensed a residually pervasive restlessness and tension under the surface—perhaps a sublimated resentment against relinquishing so many personal freedoms. Since the new rulers were well aware of the grave risks of lifting curfews and movement restrictions too quickly, they were in a quandary: How to appease the citizens' quiet but definite gnawing hunger for rescinded liberties while undertaking a restabilization program. Anarchy was a cowed wolf slinking just around the corner.

Here is where the "miracle machine" entered the march of events. This society had developed facets of advanced technology, although, curiously, this technology had heretofore been used almost exclusively for recreational and intellectual diversions. Everyday needs were met by manual labor and traditional arts and crafts. However, several cybernetic geniuses had, not long before the crisis in question developed, invented an astonishingly sensitive and complex device that could detect and monitor large areas of the electrostatic fields generated by individuals and groups. The waves or "vibrations" that registered on the monitor (not unlike our electroencephalographs) could identify in the populace psycho-physical disturbances at considerable distances. Moreover, it could pinpoint quite accurately the centers of such disturbances which could be traced to specific locations and dwellings. Crudely speaking, this "tracker" was something like a geiger-counter, only a thousand times more sophisticated. Once located, the "agitators" could be separated out of the community, isolated, and, hopefully, reformed. Their isolation chambers and rehabilitation centers were exceptionally comfortable by our standards.

For a time, this high-tech scheme for social stabilization appeared to be succeeding. All of the revolutionary unrest subsided into a collective psychic lull. Peace—or was it a heavy passivity?—became the norm. Of course, "The Detector" was not 100% efficient. But it was close; perhaps 99.99%.

After a few seasons of this new program, something became dreadfully amiss. A dense pall of apathy had enveloped everyone, everywhere. The verve, energy, and creativity that had once been the hallmarks of everyday life were somehow leaking away. Production and initiative fell to an unimaginable low. Workers were only interested in getting out of field or factory and going home. With unlit eyes, they looked neither right nor left, up or down, unless it was to avoid colliding with something. Neither incentive and austerity regimens implemented by the Directory for Social Welfare (the provisional government) nor impassioned speeches by the High Director nor sweeping promises for the future nor threatening and cajoling—nothing was able to spark new life into the people.

Agitation had been quelled, but perhaps a little agitation of some kind was sorely needed.

The High Director, who was a pragmatic humanitarian, had long been having serious misgivings about both the ethics and efficacy of the Detection Program. The Central Detection System had become a daunting and entrenched institution. As an absolute arbiter of social conformity, its actual power to influence the events and fate of the society far outstripped any individual's, including his own. What further worried the leader was that all of his subordinates seemed to be increasingly devoted to extending their own influence and less and less concerned about justice and the restoration of liberties for those they governed. He even feared that openly airing his doubts could be fatal both to himself and to the society.

The penultimate straw happened when the High Director received a demographics report that stated that the unprecedented increases in infertility, disease, and premature death had leveled off population growth. Here was the hard proof that things had gone terribly wrong. Why, the Director asked himself, couldn't The Detector have recognized this tragedy?

The High Director could not sleep that night. He decided to announce his resignation at the first appropriate time—if indeed there was to be one. But there was no one under him who could be fully trusted to safeguard the future of the citizenry. Most of the directors had turned into dedicated power-seekers. This was the crisis of crises.

The Director had a pounding headache. Though it was the middle of night, he wandered out of his dwelling like a man in a disturbing dream. His gaze was drawn to the bright night sky, his eyes scanning the canopy of spangled light. Somehow its vastness provided a peaceful perspective, a background against which he could focus on his dilemma more clearly. His headache quickly subsided.

Quite unconsciously, his head turned off to the horizon, and at ground level he saw a shimmering shadow moving in his direction. A single pulse of fear coursed through him and was gone. At fifty yards he could see that it had a definite human shape. At a few dozen yards, he could see that it was a man with a long beard. The starshine that reflected off the greybeard gave him a silverish cast.

"Greetings, brother," spoke the being when it stopped a few yards before him. The voice was benevolent but vital sounding, while the face was a wizened one with yet a youthful glow. The greybeard's eyes shone like quicksilver.

"And greetings to you, friend," returned the Director. "But who are you, and why do you greet me thus, like an apparition in the night?"

"It is not who I am," the visitor answered, "but can I help you?"

An idea fleeted through the Director's head that this could be some eccentric, if remarkable, old hermit from the nearby hills.

"No, I am not a hermit from yonder wilderness," said

the ancient. "For that is what you are thinking, and while your mind strays in such speculations I cannot help you."

"You can help me? How?" The Director, after all, had not reached his office by not questioning things. And then he reconsidered that thought.

There was an instance of silence between them that seemed to condense eons of time into a moment. The stranger's eyes appeared to become large and iridescent, taking in every facet of the Director's life and situation.

"Yes, I can help you, if you allow me to, and stop feeding your doubts with useless questions. I can help you, with the aid of this." The greybeard reached inside his garment and extracted something round and golden about the size of a small child's head. The Director saw that, in fact, it was an exquisitely molded head with all features eloquently detailed. Its lustre was the brilliance of dawn, the richness of dusk.

"You may call this the 'Head of Wisdom,'" continued the stranger. "It is a legacy of the wisest of your ancestors, of your race. I am its custodian while it is absent from you. I bring it only when it is truly needed and leave it for only that long. Such a time is now."

Hope, doubt, and questions flew around in the Director's mind. But again, these were answered before he could speak.

"Cease thinking that this is what your superstition deems a 'talisman,' and that I am an old magician come with cryptic oracles. It is not like that. The only real talisman rests on the shoulders of the wise, and its oracles are merely the words that are spoken when they must be spoken. All else is asleep and delusory. Superstition is but the ignorance of your present ways."

Then the gleaming, golden globe was handed to the Director. It felt surprisingly light in his hands. A soothing sensation spread into his arms and his body. His vision became clear, unfogged, and he suddenly felt more relaxed, more alert, and more awake than he could ever

103

remember. The feeling was echoed by the stranger's voice again.

"The head is now entrusted to you. You are to consult it only at dawn or dusk, whenever a day's thought or a night's sleep has not brought you the answer to an important problem. The Head of Wisdom will not solve your problem on command, but it will clear the confusion from your mind so that you are able to see the problem without distortion. For the real problem, the right question is more important than any answer."

The Director did not fully understand.

"You will understand when you can understand. Have patience and vigilance, and meditate upon The Head as I instruct you. The present crisis of your people was precipitated by a loss of vigilance and vision in your leaders and so in them. The time has come for your citizens to move on to a higher destiny, and the means of guidance to that destiny is now in your hands."

"When the course of your people's true destiny is fixed, I will return for The Head of Wisdom. Its wisdom will be yours, and you will then have no need of it: It merely draws out of you and reflects back the deep knowledge that is already in you but that lays forgotten in you like gold buried in mud and corruption. Peace be with you now. When I return, it will be at this hour, at this place."

The Director glanced at his timepiece. When he looked back up, the custodian of The Head of Wisdom was gone. As he started back to his dwelling place, he intuitively knew that he would not need to consult it in the morning. He knew precisely the steps he would have to take in the next few days.

In the doorway he looked out toward whence the visitor had come and sensed that the ultimate destiny of his people lay in that direction, in the stars. . . .

Ever since the Industrial Revolution several generations ago, man has discovered that technology can be harnessed and made to provide an easier and more productive life for the overworked people. And, we, who sit here typing on our wondrous typewriters and calling each other on wondrous telephones, do not deny the magic of technology. However, we may want to know if mankind is ever going to discover its "head of wisdom"—the higher workings of the mind. We have yet to comprehend, let alone acknowledge, the power and value inherent in expanded consciousness. We think we can't live without instant coffee. But what about intuition?

We spend so much time promoting technology and its parents, science and reason, that we rarely stop to ponder the many disadvantages this 20th-century family of wonders has wrought upon us. We are just beginning to realize that along with the conveniences of a new shopping mall, the environment in the area is being completely altered; that along with the manufacturing of a slick new status car comes a contribution to pollution and traffic congestion; and that along with the creation of a new weapon guaranteed to keep us safe from the Kremlin comes the threat of destroying ourselves. Science, which a century ago promised to answer most of our questions, has today given us scores of new questions and strange ideas: parallel worlds, black and white holes, time reversal, "waves of probability," interpenetrating universes, and the like. Technology, which was supposed to solve all of humanity's problems, has given us newer, more serious problems. And while it has been believed since the Age of Reason that man's sovereign intellect would find an answer to all questions, the questions have merely multiplied.

Thus, to date, our conscious, mental evolution has always lagged behind technological evolution, dragging its bags of guilt. But now that we have developed technology to the point of potential total destruction of every living thing, perhaps we've "peaked," as a drug user might say. By continuing with such heavy emphasis on technological advances, we will either grind ourselves to a halt (if we're lucky) or blast ourselves off the face of the planet. Therefore, it's time to think about our minds and increasing our mental capacities in such manners as holistic thinking, comprehensive perception, and intuition. In other words, let's strive for a bit more wisdom and vision in our lives.

There are increasing glimmers that our Western culture is beginning to explore the inner, versus outer space, as it were. True, there were the trendy 1960s, during which time *everyone* was expanding their consciousness. Executives sat cross-legged on their conference tables, meditating their way to Big Deals, while housewives studied Zen with the same fervor they reserved for ring-around-the-collar. But this trendiness did have its positive aspects. It drove home the point that having a color television with remote control and a Porsche with a megawatt stereo system that is guaranteed to render one sterile is not the end all be all. The growing, widespread interest in the relatively recent disciplines of psychology, anthropology, and sociology (human sciences) and the resurgence of attention being given to earlier cultures and ancient, Eastern systems of psychospirituality are a sign that something better is finally happening. These trends and their significance are well dealt with in several recent books, such as *The Aquarian Conspiracy* by Marilyn Ferguson, *The Turning Point* by Fritjof Capra, *Person/Planet* by Theodore Roszak, and *The Third Wave* by Alvin Toffler. All of these thinker/writers maintain that we are in the early stages of a fresh epic in world history, one signaling a quantum advance in human personal and social formation. All tend to agree that the underlying impetus appears to be psychospiritual and evolutionary in nature. This is made clear in Ferguson's book, where she contends,

> *Broader than reform, deeper than revolution, this benign conspiracy for a new human agenda has triggered the most rapid realignment in history. The great shuddering, irrevocable shift overtaking us is not a new political, religious, or philosophical system. It is a new mind . . .*[1]

106

Later in the book, Ferguson quotes Zbigniew Brzezinski, former chairman of the United States Security Council, from a *New York Times* interview (December 31, 1978), who was speaking of an "increasing yearning for something spiritual" among people everywhere in advanced Western societies, and that *traditional* religion no longer provides what we need.

> *This is why there is a search for personal religion, for direct connection with the spiritual. . . . Ultimately, every human being, once he reaches the stage of self-consciousness, wants to feel that there is some inner and deeper meaning to his existence than just being and consuming, and once he begins to feel that way, he wants his social organization to correspond to that feeling. . . . This is happening on a world scale.*[2]

Ferguson then goes on to cite a public poll by Yankelovich, Skelly, and White, that revealed that 80 percent of the respondents expressed a strong interest in "an inner search for meaning." She also refers to other polls that reveal that over 40 percent of U.S. adults report that they have had a genuine mystical experience, and that in 1978 (Gallop poll), at least 10 million Americans were engaged in some aspect of Eastern religion and 9 million in spiritual healing. Most of those involved in Eastern traditions tended to be younger adults, college educated, living on either of the two coasts, equally men and women, Catholic and Protestant, and, while unlikely to be church-goers, admit that "their religious beliefs are 'very important' in their lives." In another Gallop Poll (commissioned in 1978 by Protestant and Catholic groups) which was described by Gallop as "a severe indictment of organized religion," 86 percent of the "unchurched" and 76 percent of church-goers agreed that individuals should arrive at their beliefs outside organized religion. About 60 percent of the churchgoers agreed with this statement: "Most churches have lost the real spiritual part of religion."

Citing historians who note that most great cultural awakenings are preceded by spiritual crisis, Ferguson points out that during these cultural awakenings "there is a shift from a religion mediated by authorities to one of direct spiritual experience."

According to Ferguson, as well as the other authors cited earlier, the result of this new psychospiritual and cultural awakening is a major shift in world view that cuts across all disciplines, accompanied by a fundamental transformation of thoughts, perceptions, and values. A new human is emerging as well as a new global culture. On the analogy of the transformation of the caterpillar to the butterfly, most of these writers would undoubtedly agree that the social turmoil of our times can be seen as an external manifestation of the attempt by many people everywhere to break through their chrysalis. This chrysalis may be seen as a mental prison-shell of vanity, self-conceit, greed, ignorance, prejudice, arrogance, and self-interest, as well as many years of accumulated cultural conditioning. It also contains our obsessive fixation with technology, science, and, especially, ratiocination—our fixed "panacea beliefs."

Author Alvin Toffler describes this personal and cultural transformation phenomenon as the *Third Wave*. But he also recognizes that many people may not be able to break free of their "chrysalis"; that they are too fixated on the *Second Wave* (mass market, industrial phase) mentality. In Toffler's view, this lumbering, obsolete mentality has resulted in several interesting and popular myths that are often reflected in today's sci-fi or futuristically oriented films. "This simplistic image is based on straight-line extrapolations from Second Wave trends; specialization, maximization, and centralization." It's true. These movies often show characters in high-tech surroundings, often in command, say, of a space ship that has as many gizmos on it as New York City has taxi cabs. While these future characters are quite capable of controlling two warring planets merely by radar and computer, their personal relationships

108

and thought processes are no more advanced than Frankie
and Annette's adolescent posturings in *Beach Blanket Bingo*.
It's intriguing. While anyone with half an ounce of imagina-
tion leaps at the chance to predict what our technological
future will be, those same people are frightened to predict
what man will be like *spiritually* and *mentally* when he goes to
lunch with little green people on the planet Boing.

While Toffler speaks within the context of the myth of
the transnational corporation, he emphasizes that Second
Wave thinking does not ". . . adequately take into account
the fantastic diversity of real life conditions, the clash of
cultures, religions, and traditions in the world, the speed of
change, and the historic thrust now carrying high-
technology nations toward demassification . . ."[3]

These straight-line extrapolations are a tunnel-vision
into the future, but, then again, they do illustrate that most
of us are not yet able to use our mental powers in an *intuitive*
way. Narrowed down as they are, these Second Wave pre-
dictions come at us from all directions. Films like *Star Wars*
and *Star Trek* draw viewers into darkened theaters, promising the future, but delivering an old-fashioned Hollywood
adventure flick, replete with good guys, monsters, and a
happy ending. A bit of straight-line extrapolation? Hardly
even that. In the movie *Blade Runner,* the streets of Los
Angeles in the year 2020 are merely magnifications of today's problems: excessive noise and smog, cement as the
most common landscape material, high speed flying au-
tomobiles, and the "establishment gothic," a 700-story
pyramided office complex. The city dwellers in *Blade Runner* are anonymous, cold, and mechanical. But what about
the possibility of real human transformation? The message
is that the problems will get worse, and the technology will
get better.

Books about the future read pretty much the same.
But here, it's not only the sci-fi pulp that's at fault. The
non-fiction books on futurism also tend to be uni-
dimensional, and, while they might not feature the thrill

109

and the monster a minute that the pulpy books do, they certainly lavish a lot of ink concerning technology and its impact on us. The whether or not of the *us* involved having any impact upon our own future or even upon technology is generally ignored. For example, there is Gerard O'Neill's highly touted book, *The High Frontier*, that hypes the idea of human colonies in space as an answer to overpopulation. These colonies, which are supposed to spin about in large, donut-shaped vehicles, would be self-contained, environmentally controlled settlements, all built out of materials found on other planets. No doubt they would feature "Pac Man" and "Space Invaders" in their orbiting rumpus room. While the idea might possibly be intriguing to those who have previously contemplated vasectomies, this book's theorizing ignores the problems we still meet right here on earth—human problems. And these same humans who have overpopulated the planet are expected to remain celibate in a large, whirling donut? Will a wave of the techno-wand obliterate such problems? Again, technology is the shiny bauble we always reach for, but not for our own human mental capacities. What about settling the vast expanses of fertile but to-date uninhabited areas of the earth before we launch those space donuts?

In another popular book, *Breakthrough*, by Charles Panati, we see much of the same mentality displayed, with the usual emphasis upon medical, scientific, behavioral, and technological advances and how they "will alter the way we live" and "enhance contemporary life" in the next twenty years. As if the second will automatically follow from the first! Panati discusses computer diets, vaccines against tooth decay, drill-less dentistry, spray bandages, organ banks, do-it-yourself abortions, weather control, two-way television, tidal power, levitating trains, and, of course, space homes. Where human psychology and its contribution to the future is mentioned (under the heading "Behavior Breakthrough: How You'll Live, Work, and Love"), Panati discusses the following: rearing your baby in a controlled, "stimulus-rich" environment ("surrounding new-born infants with continuous music and color-discrimination projections"); choosing a career of crime (the latest findings on the criminal mind); sex scents (aphrodisiac-like pheronomes—insect hormones that are instrumental in mating); and hyperactive children (controlled by altering diet, room lighting conditions, clothing fabrics, etc.). Sounds pretty much like behavior by the latest manual. But, again, what about the humanistic elements? Do you want to make love to someone who is being trailed by a horny gypsy moth?

If we believe all of these *Second Wave* futurists, we are in fact heading for a neo-Orwellian existence. However, should our budding spiritual revolution indeed continue to flower into full blossom, what might we really expect the future to be like?

First of all, let's take a closer look at the Second Wave mentality—precisely where we don't want to be in the future. Persons of this type tend to be left-brained, that is, analytical, logical, and "correct," the breed particularly suited to carrying calculators in their hip pockets. Technoids. They tend to ignore the vast, unexplored territory of their right brain, as it can be too confusing and more than most can handle. They tend, therefore, to discount intuition, sensitivity, flexibility, and perception. They are acclimated to the Second Wave lifestyle, which features heavy doses of polluted air and water, Stouffer's Frozen Entrees, *Charlie's Angels,* bumper-to-bumper traffic, air conditioning, and of course, "Donkey Kong." Sound horribly empty? Unless you live in a dark cave somewhere in India, you more than likely are familiar with these things.

So what about the *New Person,* the *Ambassador of the Transformation*? What kind of person will evolve in the next few decades who will determine our future humanistic experience?

This new, transformed person will use more of his brain (namely his right brain) and will have interests that

111

will be more perceptual-varied and creative. The quality of inner states will take precedence over all else. Interpersonal relationships will also be valued, rather than status. There will be greater altruism, less selfishness, jealousy, and aggressiveness, with associated development of the more positive qualities of love, states of relaxation, liberality, flexibility, forthrightness, and altruism.

While technological advancements will continue (material values can be balanced with psychospiritual values), the objective will be to make more productive use of these advancements rather than utilize them merely for self-indulgence, war, and a mechanized existence. Instead of letting technology run rampant, we should learn to harness it in better and more healthy directions.

We will begin to alter our values, placing at a premium our mutual mental and physical health and well being, a clean and lavish environment, enjoyable, relevant, and stress-free education, interesting and meaningful employment, aesthetics, beauty, quietude, and simplification of our lives.

As the quality of our inner life is transformed in consonance with a revitalizing new *zeitgeist*, far-reaching and now unforseen (by most of us) changes in the very warp and woof of civilization will inexorably take place. Art, architecture, agriculture, applied science (including appropriate technologies), and natural resource management are examples of areas that will undergo the greatest changes in structure. Our most pressing needs today are for more human dimensions in these concerns, such as were found in certain ancient, psychologically advanced cultures. Our psychological and biological selves will be nurtured and restored to health. Instead of drab, high-rise, block buildings, we may find our future abodes more sensually and aesthetically satisfying, probably reduced in scale but more integrated with each other and fostering a more real sense of "community spirit." A return to small farming, even in "urban" environments, may occur, making locally grown

112

and wholesome foods much more available than at present. Small, independently run businesses may flourish again; in short, a decentralization of public life. And, naturally, all of these changes on the global scale can help diminish international tensions and loosen the barriers between countries and people in general.

Education as both a self-development concept and *modus operandi* is perhaps the catalytic element in all of these projected transformations. A true understanding of the learning process is an absolute prerequisite to human progress on all fronts. Critics everywhere are at this moment asking what is fundamentally wrong with institutionalized education as it is now. Answers are beginning to glimmer. A growing consensus is that learning, or the psychology of education, is somehow stuck in some medieval mental set, despite flourescent lighting, slick textbooks, and "teaching aids." What has taken the lust out of learning for so many students? In the future, education will, hopefully, once more become a pleasurable, stress-free activity that happens in the larger field of life, rather than the competitive, cerebral drudgery confined within walls that it now is.

Does this sound too utopian? Perhaps. But perhaps it sounds that way because we have been raised in such a technologically Second-Wave-oriented society, where such ruminations are frowned upon. But if the Third Wave, the Aquarian Conspiracy, and the Turning Point are inevitable, then so is an improved future picture. If you have any doubts that this *zeitgeist* is not already underway, you should read F. M. Esfandiary's *Optimism One* and *UpWingers*. For an added touch, read Edward deBono's *Future Positive* and *The Happiness Purpose*. Both authors, with refreshing optimism, point not only to a wholesome future world, but also to ongoing trends and developments that seem to be more than just a passing fad.

For example, in *Optimism One*, Esfandiary notes that although a socially integrated planet may seem very far off in the distant (if ever) future, we are *already* moving in that

113

direction but have become so accustomed to it that we rarely recognize it for what it really is:

> The oldworld which we are now outgrowing did not fragment merely individuals. Societies themselves were rigidly fragmented. Authoritarianism, patriarchy, hierarchy, feudalism, tribalism, caste, class, puritanism—all these generated their own alienation and represented obstacles to communication . . .
>
> In modern communities—for example, New York City or Copenhagen—rich and unrich, employers and employees, leaders and citizens, Catholics and Jews and Protestants and Atheists, Blacks and Whites and Yellows, Radicals and Liberals and Conservatives—all live and work and eat and drink together.
>
> Such integration was unheard of in the past. In fact the oldworld would not have allowed so many disparate groups to even live close together.[4]

We are unquestionably moving into the age of internationalism and planetary transpersonal communication. If a global mind is to emerge, that time is about here. Some writers maintain that the global mind is *already* in operation but on a subliminal level—it is only now becoming more conscious. Such was the idea put forth by psychoanalyst Karl Jung—his theory of the "collective unconscious" or the shared unconscious that exists among all members of like species.

Jung's thinking has been resurrected in the writings of such modern biologists as Sir Alister Hardy, Lyall Watson, and Rupert Sheldrake, all Englishmen. These scientists believe that the essence of the shared unconscious is psychic bonding or telepathic communication. All posit their ideas within the context of new, non-Darwinian theories of evolution. And indeed this is just what we are implying when we speak of "personal and social transformation." This transformation process is indeed evolutionary in nature and is certainly not as random or accidental as orthodox Darwinism would insist. It is more like that which the great French philosopher, Henri Bergson, implied when he spoke of Creative Evolution—a psycho-biological, transmutational progression resulting from a combination of cosmological influence in conjunction with internal, willful effort. While this is undoubtedly what is occurring in the current *zeitgeist* towards planetary consciousness, an example of the mechanism is hinted at in the following, reported by Lyall Watson:

> *Off the coast of Japan are a number of tiny islands where resident populations of macaques have been under continuous observation for more than twenty years. The scientists provide supplementary food, but the monkeys also feed themselves by digging up sweet potatoes and eating them dirt and all. This uncomfortable practice continued unchanged for many years until one day a young male monkey broke with tradition and carried his potato down to the sea where he washed it before eating it. He taught the trick to his mother, who showed it to her current mate and so the culture spread through the colony until most of them, let us say 99 monkeys, were doing it. Then one Tuesday morning at eleven, the hundredth individual acquired the habit and, within an hour, it appeared on two other islands in two physically unconnected populations of monkeys who until that moment had shown no inclination to wash their food.*
>
> *I believe that ideas in human societies spread in the same kind of way and that when enough of us hold something to be true, then it becomes true for everyone. I can see no other way in which we can reach some sort of meaningful consensus in the limited time that now seems to be at our disposal.*[5]

Perhaps, then, we should take our cue from the island monkeys and wash ourselves of the sticky debris of our Second Wave mentality. Like them, there may be many more adventurers than we know who are ready to join the spiritual revolution.

1   Ferguson, Marilyn, *The Aquarian Conspiracy*. Los Angeles: Tarcher, 1980, p. 23.

2   *Ibid,* pp. 363–364.

3   Toffler, Alvin, *The Third Wave*. New York: Morrow, 1980, p. 343.

4   Esfandiary, F. M., *Optimism One*. New York: Popular Library, 1978, pp. 55–57.

5   Watson, Lyall, in Blair, Lawrence, *Rhythms of Vision*. New York: Warner Books, 1975, pp. 15–16.

further reading

Allen, Charles L., *God's Psychiatry*. New York: Jove, 1953.

Attenborough, Richard (editor). *The Words of Gandhi*. New York: Newmarket Press, 1982.

Barrett, William, *Zen Buddhism: Selected Writings of D. T. Suzuki*. Garden City, N.Y.: Anchor/Doubleday, 1956.

Biofeld, John (Translator). *I Ching: The Book of Change*. New York: Dutton, 1968.

Bolen, Jean Shimoda. *The Tao of Psychology*. San Francisco: Harper and Row, 1979

Burtt, E. A. (Editor). *The Teachings of the Compassionate Buddha*. New York: Mentor/New American Library, 1955.

Elwood, Robert S., Jr. *Mysticism and Religion*. Englewood Cliffs, N.J.: Prentice-Hall, 1980.

Finnerty, Adam Daniel. *No More Plastic Jesus*. New York: Dutton, 1977.

Fox, Emmet. *Alter Your Life*. New York: Harper and Row, 1950.

Frye, Northrup. *The Great Code: The Bible and Literature*. New York: HBJ, 1982.

Gaer, Joseph. *How the Great Religions Began*. New York: Dodd, Mead and Co., 1929, 1956.

Glubb, Sir John. *The Life and Times of Muhammed*. New York: Stein and Day, 1971.

Hammarskjöld, Dag. *Markings*. New York: Ballantine, 1964.

Hoover, Thomas. *The Zen Experience*. New York: Plume/NAL, 1980.

James, William. *The Varieties of Religious Experience.* New York: Macmillan, 1961.

Jung, Carl G. *The Undiscovered Self.* Boston: Little, Brown and Co., 1957.

Kerocias, Jack. *Dharma Bums.* Baltimore: Penguin, 1971.

Krishnamurdi, J. *The Wholeness of Life.* San Francisco: Harper and Row, 1979.

Küng, Hans. *Does God Exist?* Garden City, N.Y.: Vintage/Doubleday, 1981.

Küng, Hans. *On Being a Christian.* New York: Pocket Books/Simon and Schuster, 1976.

Küng, Hans. *The Church.* Garden City, N.Y.: Image/Doubleday, 1976.

Kushner, Harold S. *When Bad Things Happen to Good People.* New York: Avon, 1981.

Liebman, Joshua L. *Peace of Mind.* New York: Simon and Schuster, 1946.

Merton, Thomas. *The Living Bread.* New York: Farrar, Straus, Giroux, 1956.

Needleman, Jacob. *A Sense of the Cosmos: The Encounter of Modern Science and Ancient Truth.* Garden City, N.Y.: Doubleday, 1975.

Neher, Andrew. *The Psychology of Transcendence.* Englewood Cliffs, N.J.: Spectrum/Prentice-Hall, 1980.

Nicoll, Maurice. *The New Man: An Interpretation of Some Parables and Miracles of Christ.* Baltimore: Penguin, 1973.

Peck, M. Scott. *The Road Less Traveled: A New Psychology of Love, Traditional Values and Spiritual Growth.* New York: Touchstone/Simon and Schuster, 1978.

Powell, John. *Unconditional Love.* Allen, Texas: Argus Communications, 1978.

Prabhavananda, Swami and Manchester, Frederick (Translators). *The Upanishads: Breath Of The Eternal.* New York: Mentor/New American Library, 1948.

Robinson, John, A. T. *Honest To God.* Philadelphia: Westminster Press, 1963.

Shah, Idries. *A Perfumed Scorpion.* San Francisco: Harper and Row, 1981.

Shah, Idries. *Learning How To Learn.* San Francisco: Harper and Row, 1981.

Shah, Idries. *The Sufis.* Garden City, N.Y.: Anchor/Doubleday, 1971.

Stace, Walter T. *The Teachings of the Mystics.* New York: Mentor/ New American Library, 1960.

Stein, Harry. *Ethics (And Other Liabilities): Trying To Live Right In An Amoral World.* New York: St. Martin's Press, 1982.

Swindoll, Charles R. *Three Steps Forward, Two Steps Back: Persevering Through Pressure.* New York: Bantam, 1980.

Tzu, Lao. *Tao Te Ching* (D.L.Lau, Translator). Baltimore: Penguin, 1963.

Van de Wetering. *A Glimpse of Nothingness: Experiences In An American Zen Community.* New York: Pocket Books, 1975.

Watts, Alan W. *The Spirit of Zen.* New York: Grove Press, 1958.

Williams, L. F. Ruchbrook (Editor). *Sufi Studies: East and West.* New York: Dutton, 1973.

Yogananda, Paramahansa. *Autobiography Of A Yogi.* Los Angeles: Self-Realization Fellowship, 1946.

index

Abdulla, 36
Act of Creation, The (Koestler), 39
Advertising, 10
Agnosticism, 5, 79
Alcoholism, 50, 67, 68
Allen, Woody, 33, 36, 37
Altruism, 30, 50
Anatomy of an Illness (Cousins), 38
Aquarian Conspiracy, The (Ferguson), 106–8
Arasteh, A. Reza, 93
Arrogance, 7
Art of Loving, The (Fromm), 64, 91–92
Astrology, 5
Atheism, 5, 79
Auto-eroticism, 10
Automated Lives (Langer), 44

Bateson, Gregory, 74
Battle For the Mind, The (LaHaye), 82
Behaviorism, 5, 81
Being and having, distinction between, 22–23
Beliefs, 5
Bergler, Edward, 37, 39
Bergson, Henri, 92–93, 115
Berne, Eric, 77
Blake, William, 53, 95
Boredom, 37
Breakthrough (Panati), 110
Brotherly love, 63–70
Buber, Martin, 79
Buddha, 36, 45, 86
Buddhism, 83
Burn out, 50
Buscaglia, Leo, 67–68

Calhoun, John B., 87
Capra, Fritjof, 106
Charity, 1–2, 50
Christenson, James A., 7
Civic pride, 1
Collective unconscious, 114
Coming Dark Age, The (Vacca), 21
Commitments, 81
Communism, 67
Comparison, 30
Compassion, 6–7, 49–51
Compassion (Fox), 89–90
Copernicus, 88
Competition, 18, 26–30
Compulsion, 5
Conditioning, 56–58, 97
Conformity, 57, 81
Confucianism, 83
Confucius, 67
Conscience, 51, 81
Consensual reality, 67
Contact high, 54–55
Cooperation, 30
Corporate ethics, 48
Cousins, Norman, 38
Creativity, 86–93
Crime, 28, 29, 50, 68
Crucifixion, 34–35
Culture, 50–51, 56–58
Culture of Narcissism, The (Lasch), 11
Cynicism, 40

Darwin, Charles, 89
Darwinism, 87, 90, 115
DeBono, Edward, 36, 39–41, 57–58, 113
Deception, 7, 72–74
Deikman, Arthur, 55
Delinquency, 68
Depression, 36
Detachment, 60
Disillusionment, 50
Double-bind theory, 74–75
Drug abuse, 50, 68
Drummond, Hugh, 88
Dyer, Wayne, 96–97

Earthwalk (Slater), 10, 19
Eckhards, William, 6
Education, 11, 113
Egoism, 24, 81
Ehrlich, Paul, 21
Eliot, Robert S., 15–16, 18
Ellis, Havelock, 10
Emerson, Ralph Waldo, 43, 65–66
Enculturation, 56
End of Affluence, The (Ehrlich), 21
Erotic (romantic) love, 64, 69–70
Esfandiary, F. M., 113–14
Ethical behavior, 45, 48–52
"Ethics Without the Sermon" (Nash), 48
Evolution, 89, 92–93, 115
"Evolution: Survival of the Schleps" (Drummond)
     88
Existentialism, 5

Faith, 92
Falwell, Jerry, 82
Family, 11
Fears, 91
Feelings, 32
Ferguson, Marilyn, 11, 106–8
Forbes, Malcolm, 20
Fox, Matthew, 89–90
Fragmentation, 11
Freud, Sigmund, 39, 42
Friedman, Meyer, 17–19
Friendship, 10–11
Fromm, Erich, 23–24, 34–35, 64, 66, 69–70, 80,
     91–92
Future positive (DeBono), 113
Futurism, 109–13

Galileo, 88
Games, 77
Genesis, 89
Goffman, Erving, 77
Greed, 7, 18–24, 49
Greig, J. Y. T., 37
Growth, 20–21, 92
Growth To Selfhood (Arasteh), 93

Haley, Jay, 74
Happiness Purpose, The (DeBono), 36, 40, 113
Hardy, Sir Alister, 114
Hatred, 7
Heart disease, 15–19
Hedonism, 5

Heroes, 20
High Frontier, The (O'Neill), 110
Hinduism, 83
Honesty, 7, 13, 73, 78
Hopi Indians, 50
Hostility, 7, 17, 18
Humanism, 80–85
Human Scale (Sale), 21
Humility, 92
Humor, 33–42
Hypnosis, 54, 55
Hypocrisy, 7

Idols, 5
Ik of Uganda, 50–51
Illusion, 53–55, 58–61
Impatience, 18
Independence, 31
Insecurity, 17
Insight, 39
Integration, 81
Interaction with others, 45, 46–48
Intuition, 32, 61

Jackson, Don, 74
James, 72
Jealousy, 5, 7
Jesus, 15, 23, 36
Job, 60
I John, 63
Jones, Jim, 13
Jung, Karl, 114
Justice, 7

Kappas, Katherine Hull, 38
Kierkegaard, Søren, 41
Koestler, Arthur, 34, 39
Kohlberg, Lawrence, 81

Labeling, 27
LaHaye, Tim, 82
Langer, Ellen J., 44
Lasch, Christopher, 11
Laugh After Laugh (Moody), 38
Laughter, 33–42
Laughter and the Sense of Humor (Bergler), 39
Life scripts, 77–78
Lifestyle, 16–19
Lilly, John, 5, 59
Love, 7, 37, 63–70, 91–92
Love and Guilt and the Meaning of Life (Viorst), 9
Love and Living (Merton), 82, 83
Love of God, 64, 70
Luke, 23
Lying, 72, 73

Magical Child (Pearce), 54
Male/female relationships, 68, 69–70
Man For Himself: An Inquiry Into the Psychology of Ethics (Fromm), 80
"*Many Me's of the Self Monitor, The*" (Snyder), 75
Marriage, 21–22
Maslow, Abraham, 81
Matthew, 36
McNamara, William, 83–85
Mead, Margaret, 31
Mechanism of Mind (DeBono), 57
Me generation, 10–13
Mental illness, 28, 29, 50, 68, 74
Merton, Thomas, 82, 83
Meta-systems, 57–58

Mindfulness, 44–45
Mindlessness, 44–45
Mission, 96, 97
Mohammed, 36, 70
Moody, Raymond, 38
Moon, Reverend, 13
Moral development, 81
Moral Majority, 82
Motherly love, 64, 69
Mysticism, 83–85

Narcissism, 9–12, 92
Nash, Laura L., 48
Nasrudin tales, 41
Natural selection, 28, 87
Needs, hierarchy of, 81
Neo-Platonism, 65
Neuroticism, 37
Numerology, 5

Obedience, 81
Object self, 61
Observing self, 61
Observing Self, The (Deikman), 55
O'Hare, Madelyn Murray, 5
Omnipotence, 24
Omniscience, 24
O'Neill, Gerard, 110
Optimism, 5
Optimism One (Esfandiary), 113–14
Origin of Species (Darwin), 89
Outward piety, 4
Overcompensation, 11
Oversoul, 65

Panati, Charles, 110
Patriotism, 82–83
Pearce, Joseph Chilton, 54, 55
Perception, 58
Personality types, 16–19
Person/Planet (Roszak), 106
Pessimism, 5
Physiological needs, 81
Plautus, 63
Plutomaniacs, 20
Politics, 1
Pollution, 50
Power, 19, 27
Prejudice, 7
Productiveness, 92
Psalm 22, 34–35
Psychoanalysis, 5, 81
Psychology, 80
Psychology of Laughter and Comedy, The (Greig), 37
Psychology Today, 10, 44, 75

Reality, 53–58
Religion, 79–80, 107–8
    creativity and, 88–89
    Crucifixion, 34–35
    distinction between religion and, 4–7
    humor and, 36–37
    sin and, 36
Religiosity, 4
Right livelihood, 46
Rogers, Carl R., 81
Rogers, Kenny, 20
Rogers, Mrs. Kenny, 20
Roles, 75–78, 97
Rosenman, Ray, 17–19
Roszak, Theodore, 12, 106

Safety needs, 81
Sale, Kirkpatrick, 21
Sarcasm, 40
Schizophrenia, 74
Schweitzer, Albert, 24
Scripts People Live (Steiner), 51, 77
Second Wave mentality, 108, 109, 111, 113, 115
Self-actualization, 81
Self-discovery, 13
Self-esteem needs, 81
Self-help books, 10
Self-interest, 49
Selfishness, 5, 7, 69
Self-love, 64, 69
Self-monitors, 75–77
Self-righteousness, 13
Self-understanding, 13
Service, 95–98
Shankara, 60
Sheldrake, Rupert, 114
Simulations of God (Lilly), 5
Sin, 36
Sincerity, 7, 73
Sky's the Limit, The (Dyer), 96
Slater, Philip, 10, 19–21
Snyder, Mark, 75–77
Social Darwinism, 28
Social metastasis, 10, 20
Social needs, 81
Soviet Union, 67
Spirituality, defined, 4
Sports, 11
States of Consciousness (Tart), 56
Steiner, Claude M., 51, 77
Stevenson, Robert Louis, 26
Stoicism, 5
Stress, 50, 74, 75
Sufism, 34, 41, 83

Tact, 13
Talmud, 61

Taoism, 83
Tart, Charles, 54, 55, 56, 83
Technology, 104–5, 108–12
Temper, 7
Third Wave, The (Toffler), 106, 108–9
Thoreau, Henry David, 1
Toffler, Alvin, 11, 106, 108–9
To Have Or To Be? (Fromm), 23–24, 80
Tolerance, 13
Transactional Analysis, 77, 78
Transpersonal psychology, 83
Transpersonal Psychologies (ed. Tart), 83
Truth, 65
Turning Point, The (Capra), 106
Type A Behavior and Your Heart (Friedman and Rosenman), 17
Type A behavior pattern, 16–19
Type B behavior pattern, 17, 18

Unemployment, 67
Universal Soul, 65
Unselfishness, 69
UpWingers (Esfandiary), 113

Vacca, Roberto, 21
Vanity, 7, 49
Viorst, Judith, 9
Vocation, choice of, 45–46
Voltaire, 9
Voluntary simplicity, 51–52

War, 50
Watson, Lyall, 114, 115
Wealth Addiction (Slater), 19–20
Wolfe, Tom, 11
Wordsworth, William, 99

Yarrow, Marian Radke, 50
Yoga, 83
You Shall Be As Gods (Fromm), 34–35

Zen Buddhism, 34, 36, 83